The Future of Leadership Development

Carola Hieker · John Pringle

The Future of Leadership Development

Disruption and the Impact of Megatrends

palgrave
macmillan

Carola Hieker
Richmond, The American University
in London
Richmond upon Thames, UK

University College London
London, UK

John Pringle
London, UK

ISBN 978-3-030-53543-8 ISBN 978-3-030-53544-5 (eBook)
https://doi.org/10.1007/978-3-030-53544-5

This Palgrave Macmillan imprint is published by the registered company Springer Nature Switzerland AG
The registered company address is: Gewerbestrasse 11, 6330 Cham, Switzerland

The writing of this book has given me the chance to reflect back over the last twenty-five years. During this time, my family have always been there for me, sharing the highs and the lows

I would like to thank my mother Alice and father Cliff, sadly no longer with us for their unconditional love.

My wife Maribel and my daughter Elena thank you for the support, perspective and love through the months of thinking, writing and re-writing.

Finally sharing my reflections, frustrations and hopes through the course of building this book together has been a real pleasure thank you Carola.

—John Pringle

To Michael who is always there when I need him and Anna, Sophia and Cara who I want to know that everything is possible if you believe in yourself

—Carola Hieker

Foreword

I've had a fabulous 25 years helping people grow as leaders. I'm delighted to report that I've been thrilled many times at seeing effective leadership emerge to positively impact the lives of people and contribute to the success of organisations. However, I'm afraid that the wider picture I've experienced is not so positive.

This is why this book is important and timely. Through critically reflecting on what works and what doesn't work in the leadership development industry, it gives new insights regarding which leadership development interventions will fulfil the promise to prepare and guide leaders facing the challenges of megatrends in a VUCA world.As I write this piece from my COVID-19 lockdown, I can say for sure that the nature of leading in a post-COVID-19 future will be different to what was needed twenty or fifty years ago.

To sharpen our thinking about what will be needed from leadership development in the future, Carola and John first walk us through the past features of such development, what is typical today and what needs to change for tomorrow. This certainly helped me to be clearer on how things need to be different from here into the future.

Too often, I believe that experts in the field make their input overcomplicated and difficult to digest—hence my best-selling book 'Leadership Plain and Simple'. Thankfully this book is a 'plain and simple' read that will make it easy for you to take its messages and immediately improve how you develop more of the leaders that this world needs.

Author of *Leadership: Plain and Simple*.

Rowland's Castle, UK Steve Radcliffe

Contents

List of Figures

CHAPTER 1

The Big Why—Our Narrative

Abstract This chapter introduces the central questions that prompted the book. What does the future of leadership development look like? And what needs to change in the leadership development industry that it will fulfil its purpose—to disrupt leaders in their routine and prepare them to navigate through disruptive changes such as megatrends or even pandemics. This chapter describes the urgency of the topic and provides details on how the research process was set up. It also clarifies the difference between a megatrend and a pandemic with a focus on sustainable behavioural change.

Keywords Megatrends · Change · VUCA world · COVID-19 · Future of leadership development

Anyone taking leadership in any situation needs to ask two questions:

- Why is it important?
- Why now?

In this chapter, we will share our reasons for writing this book and why we are writing it now. The why now, we will advocate, has become more distinct during the course of our writing.

C. Hieker and J. Pringle, *The Future of Leadership Development*,
https://doi.org/10.1007/978-3-030-53544-5_1

So, how did it all start? We had just run a leadership development workshop with senior leaders in a professional service firm and were meeting to catch up and informally debrief from the workshop. A major topic of the workshop had been to understand the disruptive force of megatrends for leaders, their teams, their organisation and also for the wider context. Participants of the workshop were asked to think about how their organisation and industry would need to change in the future, given these disruptive megatrends.

Megatrends disrupt human behaviour and describe sustainable behavioural change. To give some examples, globalisation, digitisation, plastic war, an ageing workforce and the changing work attitude of millennials are some of the challenges leaders are facing. However, there are also more subtle trends such as individualisation and interconnectedness (Fig. 1.1).

Enjoying our coffee, we playfully asked ourselves how we would find working with such questions if we wanted to disrupt our own leadership development industry? We are often called into challenge the thinking of our clients, to push them out of their comfort zones. What would happen if we did the same to ourselves? In a sense, we were challenging ourselves to disrupt the disruptor. Had we become too comfortable with our existing ways of developing leaders? Feedback scores from our programmes were consistently good, but as we will discuss later, this can be a seductive trap.

Our conversation had real energy and a question emerged as to whether we were developing the type of leaders needed for the VUCA world—volatile, uncertain, complex and ambiguous—in which we live? We looked across many different institutions—large businesses, politics, the public sector and the charity sector. We agreed that trust in leadership was low, which of course again prompted the question whether the leadership development industry was delivering on its promises?

At that point in the conversation we introduced the idea of writing about this topic. We shared this intention with some colleagues with whom we worked regularly. Their initial response was that so much had already been written about leadership that they questioned whether we had anything new to say—a fair challenge. However, an important distinction was made—much has been written about leadership, but relatively little about what it takes to effectively develop leaders.

So we were building momentum for our writing when the massive disruption of COVID-19 occurred.

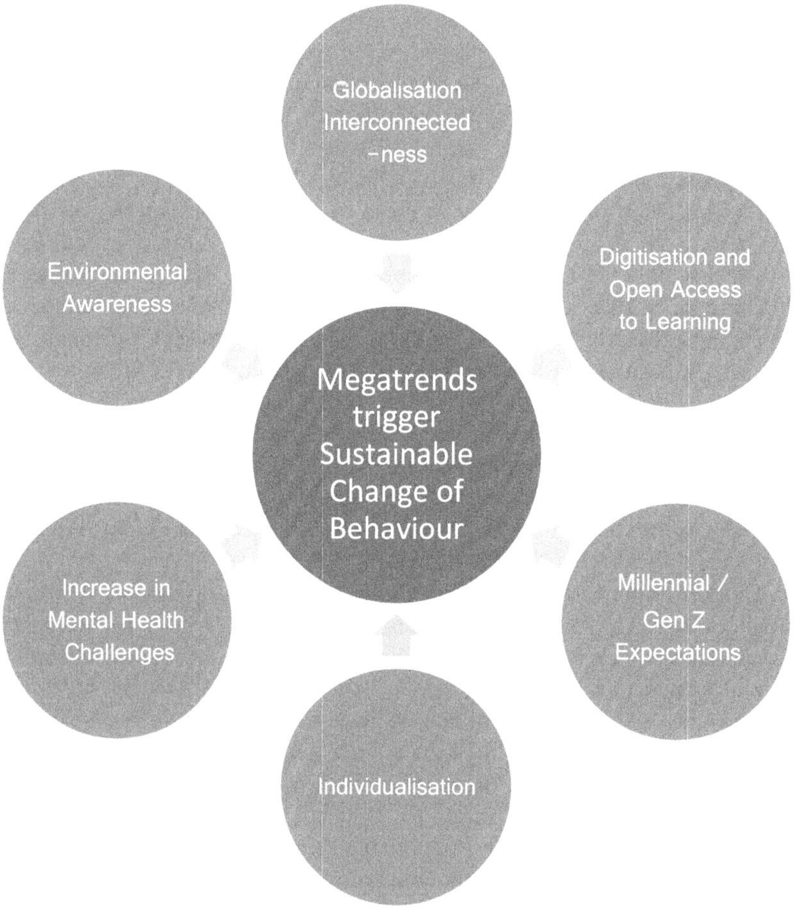

Fig. 1.1 Megatrends that have shaped our thinking

While a pandemic itself is not a megatrend, we can see that it triggers new megatrends—for example, different hygiene standards, increased online shopping, less cash transfer and increased demand for mental health support, all of which will potentially remain, even after a vaccine is found. In addition, the fast spread of the virus was triggered through a megatrend such as globalisation, and it is already accelerating existing megatrends such as digitisation (e.g. in remote working)—and there is also hope that it might reverse the megatrend of the loss of trust in experts, or reduce air-travelling to reverse climate change

A second and hugely important part of the why for this book was our own personal energy for this. Both of us have worked in the leadership development space for around 30 years. Early on in our discussions, we discussed how we wanted to spend the next period of our careers, prompting us to undertake some sense making of our experiences from the past three decades. In sharing this learning, we often experienced something of a 'deja vue' experience. 'Yes, I did this programme in the nineties... this is how system thinking influenced the landscape in Germany back then, led by thought leaders as Nicolas Luhmann or Juergen Habermas... and this what happened in London at the same time when the idea of an authentic leader became prominent with thought leaders as Goffee and Jones at the London Business School'. This discussion and sense making inspired us to write the chapter about the history of leadership development, as we felt 'looking back' helped us enormously to make sense of what was happening in the leadership development landscape and to reflect on its future.

Another source for our personal energy for writing was our commitment to learning. While we had been in the same territory for 30 years, it was also very clear that we had come at it from very different angles. One of us had focussed a great deal on the design and delivery of leadership group workshops; the other had gone much deeper into one-to-one coaching, with a huge depth of experience and knowledge about theory. As you will no doubt pick up from reading our book, we have different styles and we have not attempted to 'smooth' those out!

In writing this book, we have challenged ourselves to remain fluid and open in our thinking and conversations. In September 2019, we kicked around the phrase 'disrupting the disruptor'—who disrupts those that develop leaders to think differently? At that time, it was an interesting idea but, to be honest, we were still exploring the book from a place of comfort, getting together every few weeks and enjoying coffee together. In April 2020, as we wrote this, we were in the middle of a paradigm-shifting pandemic. Our sense of disruption was now only too acute. Leaders were asking huge questions about their own futures. There was enormous scrutiny around the performance of public leaders—a time when the only way through was to lead collectively.

Are the leaders that we have today ready? Have they been prepared in the right way for this? What was becoming clear in our view was that adjustments that people were making to the way that they work and lead would endure long beyond the peak of the pandemic.

Is leadership development ready to respond?

Our Research Process

While we believe our experience puts us in a good space to explore these topics, we also recognised that we should reach out across and beyond our existing networks for a range of different perspectives.

We decided to run formal half standardised interviews HR professionals, leadership development suppliers and senior leaders using the following guiding questions.

- What do you see as the three biggest challenges for leaders in your organisation/for the leaders in your client's organisation?
- What was the most impactful leadership development experience that you have been a part of?
- How do you see megatrends such as demographics (e.g. ageing workforce, millennials moving into leadership positions), digitisation, environmental challenges influencing the future of leadership development?
- What innovations have you seen in the delivery of leadership development which seem to work for you? What would you like to see changed?
- What do you think are the criteria of deciding for one specific supplier?
- Impact:

    For leadership suppliers:
    How do you personally measure the impact of an intervention you delivered?
    For HR Professionals:
    How do you measure the impact of an intervention in your organisation?
    For senior leaders:
    What are the best ways of measuring the impact that leadership development has?

In addition, we also talked to several senior leaders in more informal settings, sharing the idea of our book and asking them about their insights.

We will share the insights we collected during these conversations and the key themes we discovered in Chapter 4 (Fig. 1.2).

Why was there such a strong focus on millennials and Gen Z in our research? By 2025, it is expected that the millennial generation will make up 75% of the global workforce (Pathak 2019) and presently, for some professional service firms, millennials make up over two-thirds of the entire employee base. Gen Z are the generation after millennials, born after 1995, currently entering the workforce. So leadership development is not only important to foster the dialogue between the current leadership generation and their millennial teams, but leadership development also needs to be prepared to meet the needs of the next generation of leaders.

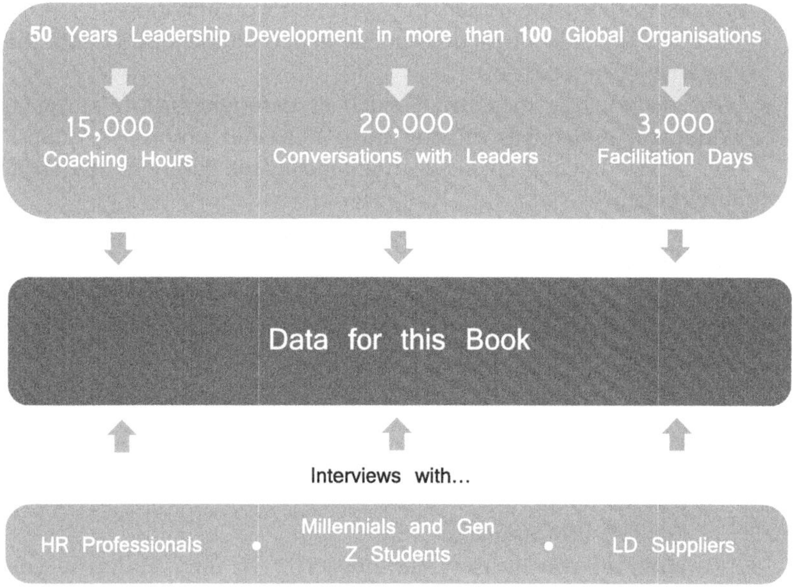

Fig. 1.2 Various sources for insights in this study

Reference

Pathak, S. (2019). Managing Millennials: A Critical Review of OD Interventions. *Associations of Indian Management Schools Journal of Management, 4*(3), 208–222.

CHAPTER 2

The History of Leadership Development

Abstract Before exploring what needs to change moving forward, it is critical to make sense of what has gone on before. This chapter outlines the history of leadership development describing the key ways in which it has evolved. The chapter maps out ten phases that leadership development has transitioned through. It begins with 'Great Man Theory' in 1927 and works through to 'Responsible leadership - the new kid on the block' in 2020. While a great deal has been written about leadership, very little has considered how leadership development has evolved. This chapter is a foundation from which readers can explore the future.

Keywords History of leadership development · Authentic leadership · Emotional intelligence · Transformational leadership · Tailor-made leadership development

The nature and form of leadership development is dependent upon the definition of leadership. In particular, it is trying to find an answer on, 'What makes an *effective* leader?' or, 'What makes a *good* leader?'

So what is leadership development? A definition we have discovered and works for many leadership development interventions we have seen was formulated by Iszatt-White and Saunders in 2017. They claim that,

C. Hieker and J. Pringle, *The Future of Leadership Development*,
https://doi.org/10.1007/978-3-030-53544-5_2

> *Leadership development is the systematic attempt to improve the wider leadership capability across an organization. This is done at a collective or group level, and requires social interaction in order to achieve an improvement in the quality of leadership.* (Iszatt-White and Saunders 2017)

However, we will later show that this definition does not go far enough, because leadership development should not simply stop on the organisational level but should indeed go further.

Understanding leadership development would seem to require some understanding of recent world history. While the nature of leadership and world history seem to be interdependent subjects—and therefore you would struggle to find any history book that does not reflect on the particular leaders of that period and what might have made them successful (or not)—not much has been written about the history of leadership development itself.

The way that leadership development is delivered to people and organisations is of course a direct result of what is perceived to be effective leadership. In turn, in order to make sense of this best-in-class leadership development, it's important to understand where this leadership development came from—what its history is, and how it evolved into a product that people consumed.

Although leadership training is just one part of leadership development, last century the focus was mainly on leadership training, moving from 'knowledge' training to behavioural training during the 1960s.

This development took place within a context where organisations moved from being viewed using a machine metaphor (as in Taylorism) to being viewed more systemically. This has in turn influenced the underpinning assumptions about how people and organisations change, and hence how learning and development interventions are designed (Fig. 2.1).

Great Man Theory—Advisors Needed

At the beginning of the last century, ideas about leadership were dominated by the 'Great Man Theory', following the idea of the Scottish philosopher Thomas Carlyle that great leaders are *born*, not *made* or *trained*. This was followed by the trait theory, and in 1927, Bingham was one of the first to formulate this view. Specifically, he held that leadership involved particular traits, e.g. being decisive, trustworthy, intelligent, communicative and motivational (House 2006).

Fig. 2.1 Changes that have occurred during the history of leadership development—in particular, how over the last decade standardised management training has moved to transformational leadership development

Accordingly, the leaders of organisations were usually also the founders of those organisations, if they had not inherited them, and were represented by the likes of John D. Rockefeller, J.P. Morgan and Henry Ford. Based on the assumption that leaders are born, there was no space for what we understand as leadership development today—there was no need for it. However, looking at leaders from this era, it has to be acknowledged that most of them came from well-off families who had invested in their children's education, as it had been the case for previous centuries, and as such critical reflection on what is required to be a good leader could have been appropriate.

In line with this, the few MBA programmes which did exist (e.g. Harvard officially started MBA education in 1908) focussed on managerial and hard skills such as accounting, finance and strategy. No explicit leadership development was offered, and even the MBA programme was not seen as critical because most business professionals felt that, in comparison with a medicine or engineering degree, it was not necessary to study business to be successful. Instead, good leaders would learn on the job.

Trait Theory—Selection Is Important

In the 1940s, the mainstream belief was still that individuals would become leaders due to their own specific traits and preferences, meaning that others were naturally less well equipped to become good leaders.

However, as a result of defining leadership traits and claiming that a leader had to be intelligent, self-confident, trustworthy and visionary (Northouse 2016), the focus shifted to developing diagnostics to find the best leader. This meant that the financial and social background of future leaders became less important. Diagnostics such as the Meyers Briggs Type Diagnostics (which was originally used to bring women into the workforce during the Second World War) began the trend in diagnosing people's preferences and leadership potential. Since then, the use of diagnostics has grown incrementally and has since become an integral part of leadership development.

Summarising the above, it can be said that in the first half of the twentieth century the belief was that a company had to simply find the right person to become a leader—rather than that most people have the potential to become leaders and with support can develop these leadership traits. This changed with the growth of behavioural leadership theories and, aligned to this, the leadership development landscape changed.

Behavioural Theory—Leadership Training Becomes a Product

This prevailing view changed in the 1960s with the idea that leaders are successful when they show certain behaviours. As a result, for the first time leadership development became of broader interest.

Not surprisingly, this was also the time when MBA programmes became more popular—for example, INSEAD based in Fontainebleau was one of the major centres in Europe offering MBA training.

A breakthrough came in 1966 with the success of McGregor's Theory X/Theory Y. This demonstrated a leadership theory which could be applied and taught, establishing the idea that leadership depends on the manager's own belief and on what motivates the people in an organisation.

McGregor claimed that managers will implement different management styles according to the beliefs they have. If a manager believes that people are extrinsically motivated, rewards and punishment are then key to influencing people's behaviour (Theory X). As a result, micromanagement and an authoritarian leadership style will be the preferred management option. In contrast, if a manager believes that people are intrinsically motivated (Theory Y), he/she will automatically prefer a more collaborative and trust-based leadership style.

While McGregor preferred 'Theory Y', he did not claim that one leadership style was better than the other. However, it is apparent that this hands-on theory was easy to train and leadership development suppliers were selling successful training courses for many years using McGregor's idea. In many cases, it opened insightful discussions and self-reflections on the leaders' individual beliefs about what motivates people, and off-site leadership training events were helpful opportunities to reflect on and share these beliefs. To a certain extent, this might also be seen as the beginnings of a reflection on unconscious bias—perhaps one of the reasons why so many of these types of training programmes were very successful and went on for many years.

Another very popular behaviour-oriented leadership theory was Blake and Mouton's Managerial Grid Model, using a framework to show a leader's 'task vs. person' orientation. On a 9 × 9 grid, this model shows on one axis the leader's concern for people, plotted against their concern for results on the others axis. Depending on the leader's focus, he/she will be less effective. Blake and Mouton (1977) claimed that managing the highest level on both scales (9/9) was the most effective leadership style and called it 'team management'. Alongside this theory, Blake and Mouton developed and sold diagnostics and built and licensed a clearly structured leadership training model which they subsequently translated into different languages and sold worldwide. While Blake and Mouton's model was first developed in the 1960s, we remember being asked to buy the licence in one of our first leadership development roles—paying the licence would have included books for all participants, a clearly structured off-site training programme, a train-the-trainer programme, and there was even an additional fee for permission for a taylor-made booklet with the key messages in German. Even though the model had its flaws, some ideas survived. The idea of balancing these often opposing challenges was picked up again by Smith in 2016, calling it 'Both/And' Leadership (Smith et al. 2016) and in many other publications positioning this as leadership paradoxes (Sheppard 2018). However, while the challenge of handling contradicting objectives is nowadays recognised as a key competence of a leader, Blake and Mouton strongly believed that there was one 'right' style which can be taught and so will make the leader successful. At that stage of leadership training, there was still the naïve belief that there was one right solution—if the leader was properly trained, then he/she would learn to apply it and be successful.

Situational Leadership—The Focus Widens

For the first time, factors beyond the importance of the leader were acknowledged, by including the situational context, as well as the maturity and status of team members.

This next significant step in leadership theory which entered the slowly growing business of leadership development was Hersey's and Blanchard's 'Situational Leadership Theory'. This claimed that successful leaders need to adapt their style according to the demands of the situation. They offered four different leadership styles, including Delegating, Supporting, Coaching and Directing. Hersey and Blanchard suggested that one of the four styles would be appropriate depending on the demands of the given situation. In addition, they offered a timeline, claiming that the chosen leadership style was dependent upon the psychological maturity of the subordinate.

While this rather prescriptive model was viewed critically from an early point by many scholars (Graef 1983), it promised very clear answers with an almost to-do list approach to the complex challenge of leadership. Without going into further details of this theory, the idea of having found the solution of what good leadership is about opened doors globally, offering leadership training as a mass-product which could be easily bought 'off the shelf'

What all these theories had in common was the promise that if a leader applied specific competencies, he/she would then become a successful leader. Leadership was seen as a competence and not a trait, so you could learn it and teach it, rather than having to be born with it innately.

Transactional Leadership—Make Leadership Predictable

Simultaneously other leadership theories gained influence, such as the Social Exchange Theory by Hollander. This basically argued that when building relationships, humans act rationally by weighing the costs against benefits—again a theory which desired to predict human behaviour and equip leaders with the knowledge of how to manage their followers' behaviour. Not surprisingly, this evolved at the same time as theories on motivation were developing, for example McClelland's theory about social motives, Herzberg's theory on motivators and hygiene factors and of course Maslow's pyramid of needs.

In leadership development terms, this meant that if leaders or future leaders understood the 'deal' and also understood what needed to be done to motivate their people, they would be successful. Many of these models, especially the motivation theories, have survived to this day. They have been picked up and slightly modified by extremely successful speakers such as Daniel Pink with his 'Autonomy, Mastery, Purpose Framework' (Pink 2011).

The Transition from Transactional to Transformational Leadership

From Manager to Leader

In the 1980s, another major change in the delivery of leadership development was established by Zaleznik in his HBR article, 'Managers and Leaders: Are they Different?' Here, he distinguished between the jobs a manager has to do and the purpose of a leader (Zaleznik 1977). In this and some later articles, he implicitly criticised most areas of leadership development run in the majority by business schools and larger organisations. He argued that at the time managerial development focussed exclusively on building competence and handling power and control, while neglecting the essential elements of leadership which include, 'inspiration, vision, and human passion' (Zaleznik 1977).

Many academics of this time, for example John Kotter, picked up on this idea—he even claimed that he had developed a 'leader vs management theory'. He emphasised that leadership was about developing a vision and strategy for an organisation, while management focussed more on the organisation of what needs to be done and the implementation of the strategy developed by the leaders (Kotter 2001).

Hence, so the theory claims, leadership can be allocated to CEOs, while management can be more appropriately tasked to the COOs of an organisation. As with all models, this is of course a simplification—no leader can survive without management, at least of his own team, and a manager without the gift of inspiring others would be a bureaucrat and not a successful leader. However, the differentiation has become common knowledge and widely accepted in business and leadership development.

So, what does this theory mean for leadership development? While, as Zaleznik rightly pointed out, in the last century leadership development mainly focussed on 'teaching managers to do the right things' to keep control of an organisation, the idea of an inspirational leader changed the landscape of leadership development.

As a consequence, the training departments in larger organisations changed their focus and leadership training became much more 'soft skill' orientated. Famously, Antoine de Saint-Exupéry said,

> If you want to build a ship, don't drum up people to collect wood and don't assign them tasks and work, but rather teach them to long for the endless immensity of the sea.

This quote was used again and again in leadership development training in the Western world to emphasise the idea that leaders need to inspire and create a vision which people can follow.

Emotional Intelligence Becomes an Accepted Leadership Trait

Looking back, both of us were already active as leadership development suppliers and HR Professionals at this time and applied much of this new thinking in the leadership development initiatives we were involved in. We felt that Zaleznik's famous differentiation, in combination with Goleman's development of the concept of emotional intelligence, started a transition from leadership *teaching* to leadership *development*. It was a quiet change in the leadership development landscape, moving away from transactional leadership development with the idea of a trainer who knows 'how to', to facilitation and coaching in a *transformational* sense—so 'let's explore together what the best leadership behaviour in this context, at this point in time, with these people around, could look like'.

However, as many before him, Goleman was still keen on developing 'leader' categories, as he did with his six leadership styles in 2000 (Goleman 2000). Similar to McGregor, he clearly judged some styles more effective than others and emphasised that the coercive and pacemaking leadership style was appropriate only in emergency situations.

Interestingly, in 2020 some of our MBA students undertook their own research on Goleman's six leadership styles and asked millennial and Gen Z undergraduates which styles they preferred. The outcome of this research supports Goleman's claim that some leadership styles are better than others (Barber and Majmudar 2020). They found that millennials and Gen Z found the coercive and pace-making leadership style the least effective, but preferred coaching to all other leadership styles. Also, we have noticed during our years of working in the leadership development area that many leaders, who consciously or unconsciously use the coercive and the pace making style on a regular basis, like to justify these by claiming that many situations in which it was applied have in fact been an emergency. Arguing in this way can be dangerous as there may be too many false alarms—if there really is a fire, nobody reacts to the alarm any more (the classic 'crying wolf' problem).

In addition, Goleman's six leadership styles were probably based on the desire to offer a fairly simple solution in leadership development—and of course, on the buyer's side, the wish of leaders to obtain simple models which they could apply and be successful with.

It can be summarised that, while Goleman's leadership styles did not survive in today's leadership development, his concept of emotional intelligence has now become an established trait and is seen as key for any successful leader.

Leadership Development Helps Leaders to 'Fit In'

At the beginning of this century, another trend occurred, the development of *leadership capabilities*. This opened the door to develop performance management systems which not only quantified the technical 'hard' skills in term of revenue, but also looked at, for example, the communication skills of a leader or their ability to handle difficult or conflicting situations. Starting with a classical Likert scale (a scale where people were rated depending on their competences between not very competent—usually 1—to very competent—a 5 or 7), many organisations built highly sophisticated performance management systems based on their respective capabilities.

These capability frameworks had several benefits. They helped the leader to understand what was seen as satisfactory, good or even better leadership. For HR professionals, they helped them judge the 'soft skills' of a leader and so include this data in the career progression of a leader. In alignment with these capability frameworks, internal assessment centres and development centres were on the rise—the first often to guarantee a fair promotion process, the latter to become as focussed as possible on areas where the leader needs to be supported. At a more senior level, these interventions were often called 'management audits' and became good business for leadership development suppliers.

For the authors and the leadership development stakeholders we interviewed, looking back it felt that, especially in larger organisations, prior to the financial crisis the leadership development world was well recognised and funded. Most (although not all) senior leaders had accepted that it was useful for them to develop their leadership skill—sometimes this was based on high self-awareness, or sometimes it was rather forcefully pushed via the above-mentioned assessments and management audits.

In combination with decent access to funding for leadership development, particularly in the western world, it was accepted 'knowledge' that sustainable leadership development should include off-site events where leaders could meet in person. Leaders needed to be supported to dedicate some time to their personal leadership development journey.

The rise of training centres which belonged to one global organisation at the end of last century/beginning of this century, as well as the building of in-house leadership academies, mirrors well the fact that leadership development had not just become a commodity, but also that organisations felt that they wanted to have tailor-made leadership development to develop their own leaders, aligned to the desired organisation's culture and values.

Summarising the different trends in leadership development over the last 60 years analysed in this chapter demonstrates that leadership development stakeholders realised over time that the concept of simple leadership solutions and 'off the shelf' products did not deliver what it had promised

Transformational Leadership and Organisational Learning

Moving away from the illusion that there is one right leadership style which can be taught and the leader will then be successful, different schools of leadership development emerged focussing on different aspects. While, for example, the Tavistock Institute and Kets de Vries at INSEAD came more from a clinical, often psychoanalytical, background (Kets de Vries 2009), applying their knowledge to the personality of a leader, others such as Peter Senge with his idea of 'The Learning Organisation' (Senge et al. 2005), or McKinsey with their 'Seven S' framework, focussed on how to change the organisation (Peters and Waterman 1982).

In a small brainstorming session with a group of leadership development experts, we identified the following trends that we have witnessed over the last 30 years (yes, indeed, there are quite a few of us who have been working in the leadership development arena for that many years!).

- from following the rules to being authentic;
- from military training to T-groups;
- from T-groups to team coaching;
- from telling to coaching;
- from training to facilitation;
- from classroom-based learning to blended learning;
- from individual to team;
- from managing to leading;
- from the same level of hierarchy to multiple-level hierarchies;
- from horizontal to vertical learning;
- from business schools to in-house academies;
- from competency framework which sits in the company to relational/collective leadership space;
- from company in-house to whole system development;
- from a hierarchical setting where leaders were at the top, to a world where leadership is expected from everybody on all levels (change agent);
- from self-development to leaving a legacy.

While each trend has influenced today's leadership development, the key trends rising at the beginning of the century (and which today would still come up explicitly or implicitly in any leadership development intervention) are the concepts of emotional intelligence (which accelerated the transition from transactional to transformational leadership—see above), and the concept of authentic leadership. Both concepts have also found a place in our language—ask any student today what is meant by an emotional intelligent leader or an authentic leader and they would have an idea of what behaviour this would include.

Another concept which has not only survived the last 20 years but was also mentioned again and again during our interviews as a key concept for leadership development in times of megatrends, was the concept of vertical leadership development (Rooke and Torbert 2005). One might argue that this is now more popular than when he first wrote his article in 2001—we will explore it further, not only in this historical section but also in a reflection about what vertical leadership development means in the current leadership development world.

Authentic Leadership

It was 1999 and we were listening to different speeches of two senior leaders. Both leaders were determined to motivate the organisation to embrace change faster, and in this particular case to make a merger work which had recently taken place between two large professional service firms. The first leader was eloquent, each movement seemed to be a good fit to what he said, all seemed fluent, and the audience was stunned by the professionalism of the speaker. Everybody agreed that this speech was convincing and that change needed to become part of the daily life of the organisation. In addition, some people in the audience secretly thought that, with his eloquence and winning words, the speaker would soon advance in his career.

The next senior leader was almost the opposite in his appearance. After a nervous smile, this person spoke about the reason why he was giving the speech, even though he didn't really like speaking in front of large audiences. Often searching for words and reflecting on what he had said during the speech, he went on to talk about his own struggle with the merger, his fears about what might happen if it didn't work out, and how even though having his own doubts he was of the firm belief that this was the right decision for the company. He was also clear that realistically the next few months—probably years—wouldn't be such a smooth walk in the park as everybody, including himself, was hoping for. He asked for patience but as well for commitment.

When he stopped talking, there was silence in the room. People were surprised by the honesty and authenticity of this leader, and instead of happily nodding and then moving to the wonderful buffet at the back of the room, they started talking, discussing their own doubts, acknowledging that smooth words looked different from the reality. For the HR professionals in the room, we felt that we had just seen a beautiful example of the power of authenticity, ably described by Goffee and Jones in their article and then later their book entitled, *Why Should Anybody Be Led By You* (Goffee and Jones 2001).

Vertical Leadership Development

Lastly, in the first decade of this century the concept of vertical leadership development became more and more accepted amongst HR professionals. Kegan's and Torbert's categories of the maturity level of senior leaders were widely discussed and fitted well with the idea of leaders leaving a legacy behind which they would then be judged on. The idea of vertical leadership development, which will be explained below in more detail, offered another angle for looking at a leader who needed to be self-aware and making sure that their actions were aligned with their values (Kegan and Lahey 2009; Rooke and Torbert 2005).

These different trends which looked at the psychology of leaders and their ethical maturity asked for special attention and invited a fairly new tool in the leadership development intervention toolbox: one-to-one coaching. The reflection on one's own positioning in the company, one's feeling, emotional intelligence, behavioural patterns and resources, limiting beliefs, autopilots, etc.—all of this entered the leader's world and in line with this coaching offered a safe one-to-one, usually face-to-face setting in which to achieve this.

Not only one-to-one coaching, but psychology itself became an accepted part of leadership development. It was in 2008, shortly before the financial crises, and one of the authors who is a trained banker and a psychologist remembers an 'aha' discussion with the CEO of a global professional service firm. They had a chat and to fit in—and therefore potentially gain new business—she pointed out that she was trained in banking and therefore would understand some of the models they discussed. However, for the first time after having worked in the leadership development field for ten years, the client surprised her by pointing out that he was not interested in her banking career because this knowledge was already available in his team. However, he *was* interested in her as a psychologist to help to reflect on what their motivators were, as well as to help them to work successfully in teams and to stop their egos getting in the way. This outspoken invitation to speak the unspeakable, to name the elephant in the room, was a new experience for her, as previously the unspoken message for most psychological interventions had been to be careful, discrete and not to push too hard.

After this intervention, we became much more outspoken about what we saw, and more confident in being the person in the room whose job it was to challenge potential group think, to ask the odd questions and to introduce topics such as responsible leadership and what this meant for the leaders' actions.

The Entrance of Neuroscience in Leadership Development

In 2008, Norman Doidge, a medical doctor and psychiatrist, wrote his best-seller *The Brain That Changes Itself* (Doidge 2008). He described the plasticity of the brain in an easy to read way and herewith made neuroscience accessible for a broader audience. His research showed that the brain can be rewired by conscious habits of thought and action, thus adding a new angle to leadership development. It showed that not just competences, behaviour and belief could be changed by training, coaching, etc., but also that some material change in the brain could be achieved. For many leadership development professionals, as for many other professionals in a 'helping profession', this was exciting news—many felt that it could finally be proven that sustainable change was possible and so with this their interventions became more credible. This neuroscience 'angle' was followed by many new trends in leadership development and triggered, amongst others, the idea of 'mindful' leadership.

A journalist named David Rock picked up this interest in neuroscience and positioned himself as an expert bringing neuroscience and leadership together. As many successful leadership development professionals before him, he developed an easy to understand model around motivation and emotion, combining it with some knowledge about how our brain works. He claimed that whenever one of the social domains—Status, Certainty, Autonomy, Relatedness and Fairness—were threatened, individuals would have a stress-reaction with the neocortex not working; whenever these social domains were rewarded, people would have best access to all of their resources. Also, by finding the acronym and calling his model 'SCARF', he made it easy for leaders to connect to his key messages and offered advice on what to do and what to avoid (Rock 2009).

The leadership development scene, always interested in new trends but especially keen on compact, nicely packed models, loved the model—and it is still in use today. As with many before him and others to come, David Rock offered an attractive combination of article and book, an easy to apply model, as well as himself as a speaker to sell this idea. This was an easy sell for HR professionals to their leaders, because it bundled a mix of interesting research, a credible speaker and a good takeaway to apply at the workplace.

Both authors have been to events where 'gurus' had been invited to speak and have witnessed how essential are the qualities of the speaker who 'owns' the model. If a mix of academic research is added to this successful leadership development product—or even better a professor from a credible business school presents the research—then the leadership development stakeholders feel safe. Not surprisingly, these 'gurus' are often able to charge high rates for their time. If it's academic, well-positioned and easy to remember, no leader will question whether this was a useful investment of their time.

Leader as a Whole Person

Over many years now, a typical leadership development off-site training event would have at least some of the following ingredients:

- Input/nuggets for wisdom, preferably some helpful leadership models which can be taken home;
- Time to reflect on one's own leadership capability, ideally supported by the results of a 360-degree feedback which can be shared with the facilitator coach and ideally with peers as well;
- A forum to meet the C-suite and establish a dialogue between the different leadership generations;
- Opportunities to exchange informally with peers and build a network;
- Some input on living healthily and an opportunity to do sport and improve physical health.

This idea of considering the 'person as a whole' and not simply focussing on their cognitive capacity was first developed by Jim Loehr and Tony Schwartz in their very successful Harvard Business Review article, 'The making of a Corporate Athlete' (Loehr and Schwarz 2001). Next to the notable and punchy title, the authors kept using the analogy of high-performance sport which resonated well with leaders who were used to working in high-performing environments. Since then, the idea that the body, the emotions, the mind and the spirit all need to be looked after has become common and accepted knowledge for most leadership development stakeholders—it is present in many variations in 'how-to' leadership books (Radcliffe and Landale 2009).

One of the most successful leadership development programmes, the authors worked as coaches and leadership development supplier in several firms with was a programme which focussed mainly on the mental and physical health of the senior leaders. It consisted of offering them advice on nutrition, sports, yoga, meditation, etc., even including doctors in the team who would take blood samples and give feedback on the leaders' health.

As this was a time-consuming and expensive intervention, not all companies kept running it after the financial crises. However, many participants the authors talk to still think it was one of the most helpful leadership development interventions that they had. Interestingly, while the programmes focussing on physical and mental health are very much appreciated by senior leaders, it seems that if a sport programme or meditation is just offered as a 'side dish' in a programme, it is often not well used. One reason might be that leaders feel that taking time for themselves and working on their health is a still a luxury, whereas phone calls and other day-to-day tasks which obviously never stop are more important. This is even more surprising, as resilience has become key for building a career and becoming a successful leader, and companies increasingly expect their leaders to look after their personal and mental health.

Responsible Leadership—The New Kid on the Block

Some weeks ago, we were asked to prepare a presentation on technology-driven change for engineers and physicists in academia. After long considerations and discussions, we decided to change the topic to 'technology-driven change and what this means for responsible leadership'. We felt that by 'personalising' technology, the tail started to wag with the dog. Even though we realise that many of us have the impression that 'technology has taken over', we wanted to emphasise that we as human beings, as change agents and as leaders, always have a choice about how to use and abuse technology.

At the end of our presentation, an insightful discussion occurred. Could a scientist in physics, engineering, medicine or other areas still fall back on 'being just an expert', or is he/she a leader per definition. During the COVID-19 pandemic, experts have become highly influential again, potentially more influential than the political leaders in charge. So, responsible leadership is not just a must for leaders but also for scientists and experts—for everybody who has influence and therefore power.

We will talk more about responsible leadership in Chapter 4—how it works, what is essential and what can be done to make it a key component of leadership development. However, some reflection is helpful at this point. There is no simple definitive model which can be applied in all situations. In vertical leadership development and in responsible leadership, it will be very difficult for inexperienced and potentially less reflected suppliers to deliver leadership development because there is no 'product' to sell. The essence of leadership development is to focus on 'holding the space', 'facilitating the dialogue', 'embracing paradox' and accepting that leadership challenges are complex—meaning that there is no 'right solution', just the best solution at this point in time.

A Final Word on the History of Leadership Development

Looking at the leadership development landscape now, the variety seems to be endless. While interventions such as what leaders can learn from horse whispering are probably still the exception, bringing in professional actors for role-play, unconscious bias training and use of sport coaches are now well accepted practise. We also see growing demand for behavioural insight scientists, influencers who help to change people's behaviour to respond to what science says. Looking at the importance of good leadership and the amount of money which is spent on leadership development, none of this is surprising.

References

Barber, J., & Majmudar, S. (2020). *Leadership Preferences: From Herzberg to Goleman*. Unpublished.

Blake, R., & Mouton, J. (1977). *The Managerial Grid: Key Orientations for Achieving Production Through People*. Houston, TX: Gulf Publishing.

Doidge, N. (2008). *The Brain That Changes Itself*. London: Penguin.

Goffee, R., & Jones, G. (2001). Why Should Anybody Be Led by You? *Harvard Business Review, 78*(5), 62–70.

Goleman, D. (2000). Leadership That Gets Results. *Harvard Business Review, 78*(2), 78–90.

Graef, C. (1983). The Situational Leadership Theory: A Critical View. *Academy of Management Review, 8*(2), 285–291.
House, R. (2006). *Culture, Leadership, and Organizations*. Thousand Oaks, CA: Sage.
Iszatt-White, M., & Saunders, C. (2017). *Leadership* [S.l.]: Oxford: Oxford University Press.
Kegan, R., & Lahey, L. L. (2009). *Immunity to Change: How to Overcome It and Unlock the Potential in Yourself and Your Organization*. Boston, MA: Harvard Business Review Press.
Kets de Vries, M. (2009). *The Leadership Mystique*. Harlow, England: Prentice Hall/Financial Times.
Kotter, J. P. (2001). What Leaders Really Do. *Harvard Business Review, 79*(11), 85–96.
Loehr, J., & Schwarz, T. (2001). The Making of a Corporate Athlete. *Harvard Business Review, 79*(1), 120–128.
Northouse, P. (2016). *Leadership* (7th ed.). London: Sage.
Peters, T., & Waterman, R. (1982). *In Search of Excellence*. New York: Harper & Row.
Pink, D. (2011). *Drive*. Edinburgh: Canongate Books.
Radcliffe, S., & Landale, A. (2009). *Future, Engage, Deliver*. Leicester, UK: Matador.
Rock, D. (2009). Managing with the Brain in Mind. *Strategy & Business, 56*, 1–10.
Rooke, D., & Torbert, W. R. (2005). Seven Transformation of Leadership. *Harvard Business Review, 83*(4), 66–76.
Senge, P., Scharmer, O., Jaworski, J., Flowers, B., & Senge, P. (2005). *Presence*. London: Nicholas Brealey Publishing.
Sheppard, B. (2018). Six Paradoxes of Leadership. *Medium* [online]. Available at: https://medium.com/@blairsheppard/six-paradoxes-of-leadership-98ef653ccae7. Accessed 16 May 2020.
Smith, W., Lewis, M., & Tushman, M. (2016). "Both/And" Leadership: Don't Worry so Much About Being Consistent. *Harvard Business Review, 94*(5), 62–70.
Zaleznik, A. (1977). Managers and Leaders: Are They Different. *Harvard Business Review, 55*(3), 67–78.

CHAPTER 3

Leadership Development—A $366 Billion Business

Abstract This chapter lays out what the authors believe leadership development is. A five-layer onion model is introduced to demonstrate the areas that leadership development professionals need to help leaders with: developing self, team, organisation, industry and the wider society. From here, the chapter addresses the size and the dynamics of the industry; the global investment in growing leaders each year is huge, which leads to many stakeholders looking to be involved. The authors explore who these stakeholders are and how they create value. The emergence of productisation and the basis on which suppliers make their buying choices are analysed. The chapter ends with the critical and long-standing question of how investors measure their return on investment in this industry.

Keywords Five layers of leadership development · Return of investment · Stakeholders of leadership development · Leadership development supplier · Leadership development buyer

A 2018 report by Training Industry.com suggested that the annual spend on leadership training is 366 billion dollars. According to data from the Chief Learning Officer of the Business Intelligence Board, nearly 95% of learning organisations either plan to increase or maintain their current investment in leadership development (Westfall 2019). Colleges and universities offer hundreds of degree courses on leadership and the

C. Hieker and J. Pringle, *The Future of Leadership Development*,
https://doi.org/10.1007/978-3-030-53544-5_3

cost of customised leadership development offerings from a top business school can reach $150,000 per person.

Yet there is mounting evidence to suggest that this huge investment is not producing the desired results. A McKinsey report (Guardian et al. 2014) stated:

> Moreover, when upward of 500 executives were asked to rank their top three human-capital priorities, leadership development was included as both a current and a future priority. Almost two-thirds of the respondents identified leadership development as their number-one concern. Only 7 per cent of senior managers polled by a UK business school think that their companies develop global leaders effectively, and around 30 percent of US companies admit that they have failed to exploit their international business opportunities fully because they lack enough leaders with the right capabilities.

If this huge investment is not working, what needs to change?

The Five Layers of Leadership Development

In our work with leaders, we often use an 'onion' model, with layers that form from the centre outwards, to demonstrate on which leadership development level the intervention takes place and how different interventions are connected. Starting from the inner circle, with leadership development focussing on the leader and their individual development needs, it moves on to the second layer which represents the team they work together with and their team development needs. The third layer reflects on the challenges of the leader in the organisation, while the fourth layer takes into consideration that any leader in an organisation is also a leader within their respective profession. Finally, the fifth layer introduces the concept that current and future leadership development cannot ignore the fact that the world is connected, and that any leader is therefore part of a wider system.

As in any model, this illustration reduces complexity and there are of course many overlaps, as will be shown in the more detailed explanation below. However, the leadership development onion helped us (and so hopefully the reader) to structure leadership development and therefore to better allocate on which layer intervention would mainly take place (Fig. 3.1).

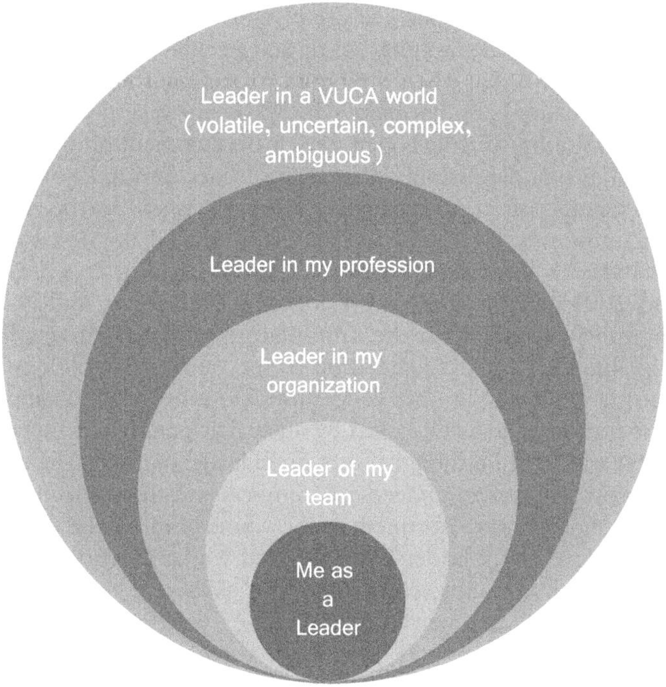

Fig. 3.1 Five layers of leadership development—the 'Leadership Development Onion'—and so the breadth which leadership development needs to cover to be fully effective

First Layer—Me as a Leader

The first layer of leadership development invites reflection on the leader as a person and aims at a higher level of self-reflection. Leaders are asked to reflect on their own strengths and development needs, to understand what their individual trigger points might be and also identify their auto-pilot start points—meaning, when do they no longer react appropriately to a situation? These reflections help to grow authenticity and emotional intelligence, which again is key in building trust. The first layer of the leadership development onion is usually where coaching takes place, as well as 360-degree feedback and diagnostics such as Firo B, Myers Briggs

Type Indicator or the Hogan—all useful tools to help better understand personality, preferences, limiting beliefs and derailers.

Our experience is that when we started working in the leadership development area, many baby boomers who were still very present in senior leadership positions, were less open for self-development on this first level. We remember one discussion with a senior leader during a so-called fire-chat—an evening often set-up by the HR department in the context of off-site training where senior leaders are invited to dialogue on different topics with more junior employees.

It was 2004 and the topic was leadership. The senior leader—a baby boomer who was aged 55 at the time—talked pleasantly about the challenges of aligning the next generation to the values of the firm and how important it was that the next generation was motivated to support the firm in its continued growth. Asked by one participant how to achieve this motivation and what he thought were good leadership skills, he answered that the main skill was to understand numbers and the company's P&L.

We as facilitators were horrified, as the whole point of the training had been about developing leadership skills, and we had focussed the whole day on personal strengths, communication skills and the art of giving feedback. Fortunately, some Gen X leaders raised their hands and were clear that this was not enough to motivate them or their team members. While the senior leader still pushed back, another Gen X leader argued that he felt that some of the company's competitors had similar good accounting skills, but he knew that clients stayed with him and his team because they valued his ability to build up rapport and trust.

This discussion shows that the first level of leadership development has come a long way. Our experience now is that almost all leaders—Gen X and even more millennial leaders—are very open to self-reflection and keen on feedback.

In the first layer of leadership development, intervention would typically involve interaction with a coach, manager, peers, trainer, etc. However, some HR professionals mentioned in our interviews that they could imagine artificial intelligence developing programmes where leaders could test reactions to certain behaviour/leadership styles, practise giving feedback in a non-threatening form, etc. The argument was that speech recognition is already available and apps are also being developed to recognise emotions in a conversation. The question is whether these can adapt to and interpret the complexity and fine-tuning of human interaction.

Second Layer—Leader of My Team

As people progress through organisations, they are often given formal accountability for leading teams. Building the team's collective leadership capability becomes an important focus. Team coaching has become a specific skill offered by consultants, both internally and externally. A variety of techniques are used in this space. Often they begin with a diagnostic phase. This can include questionnaires about team dynamics, for example Lencioni's diagnostic of the Five Dysfunctions of a Team (Lencioni 2002). They can also consist of a team version of 360-degree feedback. Pre-workshop interviews with individual team members to build themes to be explored in collective discussion are also popular.

The actual collective development intervention can take a huge variety of forms. To give some examples:

- A team-building activity focussed around a challenging task with a debrief phase;
- A workshop driven from the collective exploration of the various diagnostic tools mentioned earlier;
- The selection of an important organisational challenge to work on during the intervention, with leadership ideas being interjected as deemed useful by the facilitator;
- A structured input of team diagnostic questions that are then applied to their work situation in breakout work;
- An invitation to have non-team members come as observers to the team and provide objective feedback on dynamics;
- The sharing of personal 360-degree feedback in the team space to get additional coaching and support.

We have experienced a lot of very powerful leadership development in the team setting. The opportunity to work on real challenges the team is facing, while growing their leadership capability, gives the team a sense of progress. The opportunity for the development to be sustained beyond the workshop is also strong. Team members can reinforce the commitments made by each other.

However, there are significant challenges in this layer of the onion. Teams will often have a powerful development experience together and then subsequently a new team member will join. That team member of course does not have this shared experience that the others do. We as facilitators were privileged to be part of an experience with a team where participants shared their life stories in an outdoor setting late into the night. Huge learning and connection had been created. In the months and years to come, team members that were present would refer to the team spirit present that night as a desired benchmark. New team members would sit blankly, knowing that something powerful had happened—older team members had attempted to explain the event and their learning from it to these newcomers. However, the experiential nature of this type of team development makes later inclusion difficult.

The second challenge and often-deciding factor in whether team development is effective is the attitude of the leader of the team. In our experience, a lot of pre-work with the leader is needed to ensure that this person is role modelling the desired behaviours of personal commitment to leadership growth, vulnerability, etc. We have had a huge range of experiences in this space. On the negative side, we have had leaders who felt that they did not need to attend significant parts of the workshop, thinking that it was better to let the team talk freely without them there. On the positive side, we have experienced leaders starting workshops by demonstrating huge amounts of personal vulnerability, and in doing so creating a safe space for others to grow.

The third challenge is the fact that people are often part of multiple teams. One particular client would use an outdoor adventure experience to rebuild dysfunctional teams. One employee was a member of six different teams that were considered dysfunctional. He understandably expressed a certain weariness regarding this form of leadership development! Organisational structure charts attempt to lay out who belongs to which team, but clearly the actual way that things work is far more fluid. Deciding who should be and who should not be included can be complicated, and if not done well can create a lot of negative energy around the development experience before it has even really begun.

Third Layer—Leader in My Organisation

For many decades, the third layer has tried to answer the following questions: What is the right strategy? How do organisations allocate resources and budgets? Which organisational design works best for each organisation? What should the organisational chart look like? These are the questions business schools would traditionally focus on.

At the same time, the third layer is also the layer where companies' values need to be discussed and clarified—asking the question, 'What culture does the organisation aspire to have?' It is also at the third layer where leaders in the organisation are asked to make the shift from leading their part to asking what is best for the whole organisation. If working in a team is important, what does fair payment/renumeration look like? How can product and sales departments work closely together and handle a 'healthy' tension?

We believe that on this level leadership development can mainly add value by teaching and training about how to do things, as well as delivering new research—as you would expect business schools to do. However, equally important is leadership development suppliers adding value by facilitating the dialogue between the leaders, bringing new insights and challenging current thinking.

Considering that in most textbooks the third level was usually where leadership development would stop, we observe that the perception of leadership development is slowly changing. For example, while questions about the meaning of leadership in a broader context were rarely asked in any leadership training, over the last few decades this has now happened more and more in leadership development workshops. The fourth and fifth layers of the leadership development onion start entering the leadership development world.

Fourth Layer—Leader in My Profession

As mentioned above, textbooks indicate that the first three layers have been the focus of leadership development for many years. So, why did traditional—often business school thinking—stop here, and what do the fourth and fifth layers include?

It was 2012 and we were running a leadership development programme with the top 100 senior leaders of a global bank. We discussed in smaller groups their newly established values and their implications. All senior leaders shared their ideas about the importance of these values in the aftermath of the financial crisis, and what could be done to make them come alive for employees of the organisation. Suddenly, one senior leader got rather angry and said that he was tired of being the 'bad guy' of society. He had stopped sharing at social events that he was a banker, as people often seemed to blame him personally for losses they made during the financial crisis and that he found it really difficult to handle people's anger. This started a very insightful discussion about what it meant to be a representative of a profession, and that it was not good enough to only try to improve one's own organisation—rather, the whole profession had to bundle resources together to attempt to change behaviours and perception in society.

However, we all know that the gap between intention and action is difficult to close. It might be due to the fact that the competition between the key players in one profession is more powerful than seeing the need to contribute to the whole of that profession. It might also be, as Brookes' points out, that leaders need to be selfless to lead collectively, something which can be difficult in a competitive world (Brookes 2015).

Today, the challenge is a similar one for the large technology companies such as Facebook and Google. The Cambridge Analytica scandal shocked society, and as the journalist Carole Cadwalladr expresses well 2019 in her TED talk, the 'Gods of Silicon Valley' need to act, take responsibility and show collective leadership.

While the third layer leadership development supports leaders to move from 'me and my team' to the organisation as whole, the fourth layer shows that something such as 'the good bank' or the 'good technology company' does not exist. Leadership for a whole profession is needed, and so again leadership development's role is to support the dialogue, bring new research and challenge 'silo' thinking.

Fifth Layer—Leader in a VUCA World

In the global world that we live in, the boundary between level four and level five becomes more and more blurred. Consider that Facebook now does financial services and is moving further into that realm, or that Google is archiving huge amounts of books and literature, turning itself into a mega-library… it is no longer sufficient to take leadership in a profession without taking leadership on a broader scale.

During a leadership programme recently run by the authors, a participant jokingly said, 'I read that CEO doesn't stand for Chief Executive Officer any more, but for Chief Ecosystem Officer'. This started an intense discussion in this particular group of leaders about how they felt overwhelmed by the topic of climate change. They felt that they were now responsible for solving this problem, but at the same time they did not have any ideas about how to do this. Some participants started blaming different countries and politicians who had sacrificed environment guidelines to improve their economy, until one participant said, 'Why don't we start with us and our employees?' Even though it is just one small step, what can we do to inspire our employees to have a careful look at how they are producing waste inside and outside the workplace? How can we reduce emissions related to company's travel even further, without sacrificing the feeling of community and belonging, etc.?

This example illustrates well that at this outer circle of leadership development the discussion very quickly becomes abstract and leaders revert to observer mode. Judging how well-researched the presentation of the latest climate change statistics are, and potentially how well prepared the facilitator introducing megatrends and the VUCA world might be, the twist in the above example shows that the moment the fifth layer was brought back into their world, it became real—change was tangible and the mindset shifted from that of spectator to that of change-maker, from consumer to contributor, from being affected to being involved. For us facilitators, this was almost a magical moment—change happened in the room in the best sense of leadership development.

Since the outbreak of the COVID-19 pandemic, people have started seeing that walls and boundaries can't stop a pandemic. Inequality and diseases need to be combatted; clean water and health care need to be sought for everybody—these are the priorities that need to be tackled to protect our health and wealth. These are the topics which need to be 'brought into the room' at the fifth layer of leadership development.

The Key Stakeholders of Leadership Development and Their Agendas

As we have discussed, leadership development grew over the decades incrementally until it became a huge global business that it is today. Reflecting on the five layers of leadership development, it is even more interesting to think about who the stakeholders are and what their agenda might be. From our perspective, the following players are always either directly or indirectly involved in any leadership development intervention:

- Leader;
- Leader's line manager;
- Senior leadership team;
- The HR professional/internal consultant;
- The owner of the business/the investors in the business;
- The leadership development supplier (facilitator, coach, trainer ...) (Fig. 3.2).

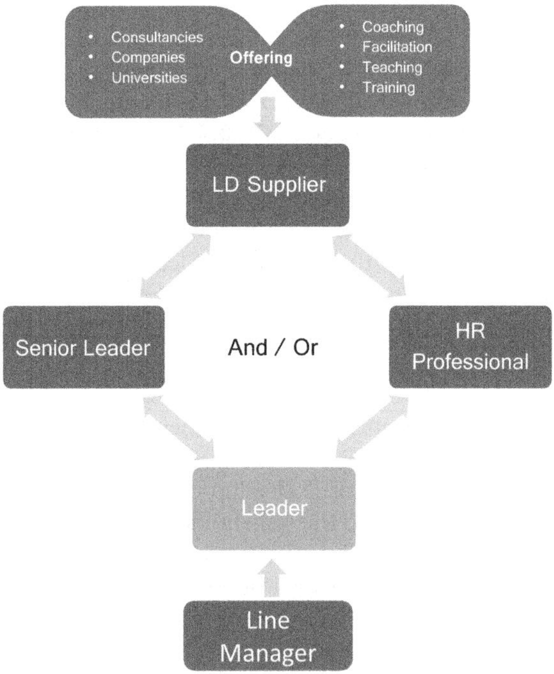

Fig. 3.2 Flow between different stakeholders in typical leadership development interventions and the range of the offering

The Supply Side

Given the size of the industry in terms of value, it is natural that it has become a highly competitive space—there are quite a range of organisations competing for a slice of the cake, including:

- Business schools;
- Large consulting companies cross-selling on the back of large organisational transformation programmes;
- Consultancies offering to manage the whole backroom operation around learning and development for clients;
- Head-hunters offering ancillary services;
- In-house academies;
- Niche consultancies specialising in the area;
- And a phenomenon which we have called 'gurus'.

In addition, the range of people working in the space from different disciplines has grown dramatically. Clinical psychologists, actors, musicians, sportspeople, hostage negotiators, comedy improvisation performers, horse whisperers and ex-military people have all moved into this lucrative space.

Gurus

One interesting manifestation of the enormous opportunity provided by the size of the leadership development market is the presence of so-called gurus. Typically, the guru either develops a big idea or picks a good (but not well-known) leadership development model and packages it for the market. Often that packaging takes the form of a book, followed by a lecture tour, or in more recent times, a TED talk. The Guru then scales the training and licenses it to others to use the brand or the big idea, utilising a franchise model. An obvious example of this would be Steven Covey's *Seven Habits of Highly Effective People* (1990s). Today, there are hundreds of thousands of licensed trainers who will guide individuals and groups through the model.

These gurus often provide a framework and common language that can be scaled throughout an organisation—hence the appeal to the buyer. At a more personal level, people are then attracted to the simplicity and reassurance that a framework provides. The thinking is that if I apply this to my leadership, then success will follow.

Without doubt, many of these frameworks and big ideas provide some useful thoughts and practices for leaders as they develop. The question is, how do these frameworks stand up to the type of VUCA world that leaders are trying to lead within? The challenges thrown at leaders are often highly complex and many of these frameworks, if followed in a rigid way, can actually take leaders down the wrong path. Over the years, we have used many of these frameworks in our own work. Increasingly though, it has proved useful to encourage leaders to hold these structures lightly, framing them more as lenses through which to look at a situation, rather than as a set of fixed steps.

A question for the leadership development industry will be how these gurus fare moving forward. Clearly, the immediate accessibility of ideas and videos means that many potential buyers feel that they do not need to pay for the book or the live lecture. However, the ideas themselves still play a part in face-to-face workshops. Designers of such workshops will assume that people are coming to the training having researched the idea and prepared to work with it on live organisational challenges. This will dramatically change the balance of how time is spent during these workshops, providing less input and allowing more time for exploration.

This presents a major challenge to the gurus themselves and the people they train in their product. The skills needed to take people through an entertaining, often PowerPoint-led idea, are very different from the facilitation skills needed to work with a live conversation. Live conversations have the potential to leave the safety of the 'model' and branch off into many different areas of thought. Do the gurus have the range of tools to successfully lead that, or do they often unhelpfully bring it back to the model they have developed?

To give a real example, a guru was presenting their idea to a large group of leaders in an organisation. It became clear after 20 minutes that the participants had got the essence of the model and wanted to apply it to their business challenges. The guru ploughed on adding more layers to their model. The audience became distracted, phones started to emerge and quite a number of participants left the room. At the lunch break, we tried to engage the guru in a conversation about how the session was going. The guru's response was to defend the model and the need to spend more time explaining it.

What drove this behaviour in the guru? Perhaps a fear of not being able to cope with a live conversation, or a concern that they were undermining the credibility of their own model by moving away from it. It could have been a lack of preparation as to how they would handle a live conversation from a design and learning outcomes perspective… or all three may have been true. This can occur despite the best efforts of internal programme designers who have often briefed the guru on the organisation and the interactions they would like to see. Many of these gurus seem to believe that their brand and the stock stories they tell will be enough to carry the day.

Many gurus are not active organisational consultants and the lecture tour is not the same as actively working with clients. The danger is that their ideas are somehow concepts which have not been rigorously tested in the field of organisational action. They may have been developed through research interviews, but this is very different from the live testing and reshaping of ideas on client projects.

We had the privilege of being part of the development of a new leadership framework called 4i (Landale and Lock 2019), which took over three years to build as it was formed on the basis of live client interactions. To use a phrase, 'flying the plane and building it at the same time', some gurus and clients may find that far too risky a proposition—but in our experience it is far more congruent with how leaders need to be developed to meet current challenges.

It is also likely that the lifespan of gurus and their ideas will shorten. The accessibility that people have today to new ideas means that people will move on much more quickly. We have explored your idea, now what's next? Gurus will need to prove faster at reinventing themselves or finding a new angle on existing ideas. However, that angle will need to be a genuine development, rather than a repackaging, as audiences have become more discerning as their exposure to this market has increased. The guru space is now a highly competitive one, particularly if the target audience consists of millennials. Traditional gurus are competing with Facebook influencers, Vloggers, YouTube stars, etc.

Naturally, guru's ideas will always have a certain lifespan. Leading-edge companies and iconic business leaders often become outdated, either because the market has moved on, or perhaps because history has discredited their approach. Fred Goodwin, CEO of RBS, was once cited as a role model leader. Today, he is described as an egotistical leader who nearly brought down the world's financial system.

To be sustainably successful, gurus will need to be highly savvy with how they use social media. With such high levels of exposure, there needs to be congruence between their public and private personas, as both are often visible through social media. In an area as personal as developing as leaders, buyers will be dismissive if they believe that gurus are not living their brands.

This then leads to a bewildering series of choices for the buyers. Buyers naturally search for some criteria on which to make their purchasing decisions. Qualifications would naturally be one place to look. However, leadership development is a very fragmented space, and there are very few standard benchmark qualifications. Some have tried to create qualifications within the executive coaching space—indeed, buying organisations have often created their own assessment processes, for example for executive coaches.

Buyers and How Do They Choose?

The leadership development supplier faces many buyers who are not usually aligned amongst themselves and who make judgements from a consumer perspective. In our experience, one significant tension that the supplier faces is the lack of respect felt for the HR function within the business. Learning and development is clearly a specialism within the HR function. Our experience would suggest that these roles are often occupied by people who are HR generalists obtaining some experience in the area before then returning to more general roles. This means that they often lack the experience and depth of knowledge to judge the real quality of what is being offered by suppliers.

Another trend we have seen (and we are also part of) is that leadership development professionals who work in an organisation may do so for a number of years before then establishing their own leadership development consultancy. This has led to a number of occasions when earlier interactions between the organisation and the suppliers have simply bypassed the HR function. This often leaves the supplier with the tricky task of placating an isolated HR function further down the line, when contracts and formal processes have started to kick in.

One more challenge is that the HR professionals often see themselves as 'gatekeepers', yet they might not have the level of discussion with the senior leader to create something together which is best for the business.

A poignant example of this was a team development workshop in the USA. Three members of the HR function arrived on the morning of the first day, announcing that they were there to evaluate the workshop as it unfolded. Their request was to sit outside the circle of participants and type notes on their laptops. This request was refused by the supplier. The interesting question is really about how we got to this situation—for us some of the answers lie in the dynamics described above.

Due to these various issues, buying decisions are often made on the basis of two factors. If the organisation has significant resources for learning and development, then they may play it safe and employ a well-branded supplier. This safeguards the buyer from criticism in the organisation should the development programme fail. It certainly explains the fact that not only in strategic consulting, but also in leadership development, large consultancies or headhunting companies often win the contract, despite submitting the most expensive proposal.

Alternatively, they may go with a supplier that they know and trust from recommendation or previous experience. This of course is a good starting point, but can also lead to a lack of objectivity in the decision-making process. It can also lead to a lack of freshness of approach, as the suppliers themselves may have become 'part of the furniture' of the organisation. Challenging suppliers as to how they are remaining objective to the culture that they are working in is an important question that buyers could ask.

We have seen a number of occasions where real experience has been built within organisations. The challenge is retaining this experience and keeping the experienced internal leadership development professionals on board, as the supplier side can often appear more attractive than the buying side.

Productisation

The response to this huge commercial opportunity and the global nature of many of the buying organisations have been for suppliers to create standardised products that can then be scaled. The range of products being provided by the suppliers is diverse, including:

- Traditional classroom-based PowerPoint with some group breakout work;
- E-learning packages;
- One-to-one coaching;
- Team coaching;
- Team building experiences;
- Leadership retreats;

- Action learning;
- Executive assessment centres;
- Psychometric tools;
- Leadership conferences;
- Leadership journeys;
- Leadership competency frameworks.

Some buying organisations have welcomed this plurality, as it offers a chance to create some common language around leadership in their organisations. It has also reduced the cost of customisation. However, the productisation has also come at a cost. Leadership is ultimately personal, in the sense that individuals bring themselves to leading, which does not fit well with standardised development products. Many leadership development products are characterised by PowerPoint presentations illustrating leadership models, which therefore create a sense of the right answer. There is also a sense that these products reinforce the leader as consumer rather than driver of their own development—something that we will explore later. This productisation also allows suppliers to employ people with relatively low skill to deliver the training at low cost, creating larger margins for the owner of the supplier companies.

The unpredictable nature of the world that leaders have to navigate does not correlate to these standardised leadership development products. In our experience, when conversations broaden and deviate from the standard models, these cheaper and less skilled facilitators are unable to cope with the ambiguity. The participants who are really engaged sense this and become disengaged.

Finally, standardised leadership development products often do not work because they bump into a huge variable across all organisations—culture. A quote often attributed to Peter Drucker reads, ‘Culture eats strategy for breakfast’. In our experience, this has a massive impact when trying to apply a leadership development approach that worked well in one organisation to another (Campbell et al. 2011).

Sometimes pieces of language that are embedded in these products lead to immediate rejection. One example we experienced was the use of the words ‘let’s build a leadership community across the organisation’. There were audible groans across the conference room, ten minutes into the first workshop. Deeper investigation after the workshop provided insight into why the word ‘community’ was received in this way. Much of it was linked to a now-discredited leader who had taken the organisation down an unhelpful path.

Starting with the Product or the Need?

In our early working lives, we came across a company using an approach called the 'Learning Value Chain'. This was a rigorous process which guided all parties involved in building a leadership development intervention. It started by encouraging those involved to identify the business need to be addressed by the development. This was followed by questions about how that then translated into learning needs for the target audience. Only then could conversations about learning design begin. While this process might look rather rigorous, alignment with the business is powerful and helps the intervention remain focussed—very much in contrast to our experience of how leadership development interventions are usually built.

On too many occasions, suppliers start with the products and services they have built and then, if required, customise the product to the client situation. This view is backed up by Ray Williams who explains that this is one of the reasons 'Why leadership development programmes fail' (Williams 2019).

> Leadership development consultants often try to offer a Chinese menu of leadership insights, based on their work instead of the context that looks at the work of the company. The challenge for leadership development? Having the clarity to offer the two or three things that matter most to the organization, not just the 46 things (or 21 irrefutable laws) that look like leadership.

Business schools offering MBA programmes could also ask themselves the same question. Are they really preparing leaders for the challenges that organisations are facing into the future, or are they teaching the content that they have researched?

A piece of PwC research (PwC 2019) suggested that the following were the top ten threats that CEOS felt their organisations faced:

- Uncertain economic growth—82%;
- Over-regulation—80%;
- Availability of key skills—77%;
- Geopolitical uncertainty—74%;

- Speed of technological change—70%;
- Exchange rate volatility—70%;
- Increasing tax burden—68%;
- Social instability—68%;
- Changing consumer behaviour—65%;
- Cyber threats—61%.

To what extent do the leadership development programmes provided by the range of suppliers described prepare leaders for the challenges described above?

Licensing and Qualifications

One of the by-products of the rise in productisation of leadership development has been a proliferation of qualifications and licensing around 'copyrighted' material.

Let's start with licensing. This is when a supplier has developed an idea, perhaps a leadership model or framework, which it then copyrights. Often this framework will have been introduced into a client via a supplier's leadership development facilitator/trainer. The client then often wants to use the framework outside of occasions when the supplier is present. The supplier will ask for a licence fee to use it and frequently charges to train internal people in how to use the framework. This can be attractive to both parties, as internal trainers are often much cheaper than external ones. An example of this approach being used very successfully is 'Steven Covey's Seven Habits of Highly Effective People' (Covey 1989)—there are hundreds of thousands licensed trainers qualified to use the framework.

One supplier organisation that we worked with even told us that they had made more money from litigation suits filed against organisations using their copyrighted material, than they did from consulting fees!

However, the question for the future is whether this model will endure. Digitisation has meant that these frameworks and models are widely available on the web alongside direct teaching from those who developed them. The longevity of gurus and their frameworks is also becoming shorter, as channels such as YouTube and TED have significantly reduced the barriers to entry for newcomers. The previous model often worked because of an established book placed with a reputable publisher which had been well marketed over a period of time. Our experience is that clients no longer feel that the differentiator is the framework or the material. In fact, leaders often now express fatigue concerning the production of yet another framework. They are seeing that the real value is in skilled facilitators who can bring a wide variety of these tools and frameworks to real organisational challenges as and when they are required.

Secondly, let's explore supplier qualifications. A wide variety of training programmes have been provided, primarily by business schools and coaching academies, offering a qualification at the end. The most prominent area for this has been in the executive coaching market. Building a qualifications framework that is widely recognised has some real potential benefits. Many other professions, such as accountancy, medicine, engineering and law, have all built their credibility around such qualifications. The leadership development market is a highly fragmented one, with many different organisations involved. This has meant that it has been difficult to build consensus around which qualifications are the ones practitioners should strive to attain.

In our experience, clients buying services in the leadership development space would like to be able to ask for widely recognised qualifications as part of the selection process. As we have discussed elsewhere, huge amounts of money are being spent, and so qualifications may offer some assurance that these investments are well made. However, in the main this has not happened, meaning that clients have often resorted to building their own selection methods for suppliers. In fact, during our time on the buying side, we were personally involved in assessment centres for executive coaches.

Moving forward, the growing trend that leadership development is more individualised, and with material widely available via digitisation, we feel that licensing and qualifications will not be a major part of the future for leadership development. Consumers of leadership development will largely make their buying decisions on relationship and trust, often generated by the recommendations of others.

How to Measure Success—The ROI?

One of us finished her PhD in 1995, titled, 'How to evaluate communication – and behavioural training in organisations – an empirical study in financial services' (Hieker 1996). The study collected pre- and post-training data directly after the training and several weeks later. It included self-perception, but in addition the superior of the participant was asked whether they had noticed any positive changes aligned with the training objectives. After three years of intensive literature review, as well as collecting empirical data, applying statistics and calculating path analysis to find correlation to explore the ROI of the so-called soft skill trainings, one would think that the author should be proud of the expertise gained in one field and be ready to apply the results in practice.

However, almost the contrary was the case. It felt the more research was done in the field, the more difficult it was to come to one succinct conclusion. Too many variables influenced the outcome of the study, beginning with key criteria such as the quality of the training, the quality of the facilitator and how useful the participants found the content at this stage of their career. While these are certainly important criteria to determine the success of an leadership development intervention, other more random variables existed, including how participants got along with other participants, whether they liked the facilitator or the location, even up to whether they liked the food or if the weather was fine. All of these influenced the results, especially the feedback collected directly after the training. As most leadership development interventions we were running at this stage (and unfortunately this is still the case) focus mainly on these 'happy sheets' collecting standardised participants' feedback after the training, for many years now we have stepped back from the wish to prove the ROI of leadership development intervention.

However, in 2004 we were involved in a leadership programme for the third-level leaders in an insurance company. The programme itself included a lot of best-in-class features for high potential trainings—on the job training, development workshops, peer feedback, allocating mentors and individual coaching. Also, ROI was taken seriously, and the company was ready to invest time and resources to not just develop these leaders but also track the success of the programme. Programme and individual objectives were agreed between key stakeholders at the start and at the end of the programme. Several months later interviews with all stakeholders, as well as participants, were conducted in order to understand what had changed and how far the company benefitted from these changes—financially and otherwise. The outcome was astonishing. Of course, no evaluation of behavioural change will ever be completely expressed in hard numbers, but it was amazing reflecting how much the company had earned due to, for example, the cooperation between two business units which grew out of a project triggered by this high potential programme.

This experience is aligned with Kirkpatrick's suggestion (Kirkpatrick and Kirkpatrick 1994) that there are four levels in which we can measure the effectiveness of outcomes of learning interventions.

- Immediate reaction—happy sheets!
- Pre- and post-intervention knowledge measures;
- Behavioural change after six months—pre and post use of 360-degree feedback would be an example;
- Business results—much harder of course to link in terms of cause and effect with learning interventions.

We strongly believe that if companies continue to put significant effort into measuring outcomes, it will help to recognise the multifaceted nature of leadership development and also help to increase the trust that investments will bear fruit.

Meanwhile, just going along with the traditional and easily collected 'happy sheets' at the end of a programme could be counterproductive to real development, as this in fact drives safe behaviours on the part of HR departments and suppliers. HR professionals and HR suppliers need to be ready to take a risk in a VUCA world—if 'off the shelf' solutions do not exist anymore, and leadership development has to step (or sometimes be pushed) out of one's comfort zone, it is necessary to take the complexity of any change into consideration to prove ROI.

References

Brookes, S. (2015). *The Selfless Leader: A Compass for Collective Leadership*. London: Palgrave Macmillan.

Campbell, D., et al. (2011). *Business Strategy: An Introduction*. Basingstoke: Macmillan International Higher Education, 1 April 2011. Accessed 10 January 2020.

Covey, S. (1989). *The Seven Habits of Highly Effective People*. New York: Simon & Schuster.

Guardian, P., Halbeisen, T., & Lane, K. (2014). *Why Leadership-Development Programs Fail* [online]. McKinsey & Company. Available at: https://www.mckinsey.com/featured-insights/leadership/why-leadership-development-programs-fail. Accessed 21 March 2020.

Hieker, C. (1996). *Evaluation von Kommunikations- und Verhaltenstraining in the Workplace*. Aachen: Shaker.

Kirkpatrick, D. L., & Kirkpatrick, J. D. (1994). *Evaluating Training Programs*, 1333. Broadway, Oakland: Berrett-Koehler Publishers.
Landale, A., & Lock, I. (2019). *4i Leadership: How to Start a Bolder Conversation*. Anthony Landale & Ian Lock.
Lencioni, Patrick. (2002). *The Five Dysfunctions of a Team*. San Francisco: Jossey-Bass.
PwC Ceo Survey. (2019). https://www.pwc.com/gx/en/ceo-survey/2019/report/pwc-22nd-annual-global-ceo-survey.pdf. Accessed 13 February 2020.
Westfall, C. (2019). *Leadership Development Is a $366 Billion Industry: Here's Why Most Programs Don't Work*. https://www.forbes.com/sites/chriswestfall/2019/06/20/leadership-development-why-most-programs-dont-work/#2e66935d61de. Accessed 10 December 2019.
Williams, R. (2019). https://raywilliams.ca/why-leadership-development-programs-fail/. Accessed 18 March 2020.

CHAPTER 4

Question Time with Key Stakeholders—The Future of Leadership Development

Abstract The authors have over 50 years of development experience between them. To supplement this experience in the field, they conducted interviews with stakeholders from across the leadership development industry. As a result, three frameworks are seen as key to develop leaders to be best prepared for disruptive changes: responsible leadership, vertical leadership development and building collective leadership. Recommended tools to sustainably support leaders are coaching, 360 feedback, action learning, shadow coaching and mentoring. Insights are also offered as to what may get in the way of the changes that are needed: leaders behaving as consumers, suppliers playing it too safe and a lack of diversity in those contributing.

Keywords Vertical leadership development · Responsible leadership · Collective leadership · Coaching · Action learning

For our empirical research, we conducted half-standardised interviews with twenty HR professionals and ten leadership development suppliers which usually ran for an hour.

In addition, we talked to around 20 senior leaders, this time in more informal settings, about what they thought was the influence of mega-trends on leadership development, what was working within leadership development, and what needed to be changed.

C. Hieker and J. Pringle, *The Future of Leadership Development*,
https://doi.org/10.1007/978-3-030-53544-5_4

In all interviews, both formal and more informal ones, we declared our intention to use the information for our research, making clear that all the data would be anonymised and subsequently published in this book.

Finally, we asked students who are either millennials or Gen Z, what they expected from a leader of an organisation, and how they would like to be developed to become a leader.

On a methodological note, we want to emphasise that we are aware that we used opportunistic sampling (Bell et al. 2019). However, we believe that because most of the HR professionals we talked to work in global roles, as do the leaders, the cohort therefore has good insight into the topic of global leadership development. In addition, because the students we talked to come from Europe, USA, the Middle East and India, and because they reached out to millennials in these different regions, we believe that the results represent patterns regarding leadership development which you would find globally.

The three megatrends mentioned most frequently in these different contexts were the different work perspective of millennials, digitisation and the rising awareness of climate change. This was before the onset of the COVID-19 crisis, after which all conversations were about leadership in the midst of a pandemic. We discussed whether this new large megatrend had influences different from the other ones, and felt that the findings were emphasised with more urgency and emergency.

Unanimously, all interviewees agreed that leadership development should not be about offering solutions and models, pretending that with the right application of the same the leader would be successful.

The metaphor, 'leadership development is like going to the gym – you don't build up muscles by watching the instructor', suitably demonstrates that the success of leadership development is dependent on the attitude of the leader to be willing to learn, reflect critically on himself/herself and probably even more importantly, their willingness to unlearn.

When asked about the most powerful leadership development experience they ever had, all leaders, HR professionals and HR suppliers were clear that it was an event where leaders were pushed out of their comfort zone, forced to reconsider comfortable narratives or to discover own limiting beliefs. In addition, there was a unanimous voice that these powerful leadership development experiences were never just a 'one-off event', but rather initiatives that were embedded within a process which continued in the day-to-day job.

One-to-one coaching was mentioned frequently as key to the leader discovering their unhealthy patterns and also instrumental to implement a sustainable change and stop the 'autopilot'—as one of the interviewees called it.

Many of the messages we heard from the HR professionals and the senior leaders were also repeated by the millennials. Across several studies, millennials stated that one-to-one coaching was a key element of leadership development for them and that they expected coaching and mentoring at the workplace (Hieker 2019).

The students also believed that everybody could gain leadership skills and that this should be offered by companies on an ongoing basis. However, in contrast to former research that showed that millennials require technology to remain motivated in their learning (Ben-Hur and Ringwood 2017), the majority of millennials in our research valued face-to-face training over and above online training or relevant reading. Some millennials also emphasised the aspect of on the job learning, stating that they needed more practical training and were keen on having more responsibility, which would, in turn, help them to develop their leadership skills.

Asked about what they were expecting from a good leader, the highest rated attributes were team orientation, empathy and intercultural communication, followed by giving guidance and support. This support would include clarity on their role and their future development, and receiving constructive feedback on an ongoing basis. Probably, the most interesting finding of the research was that 97% of the millennials who took part were clear that if there was a lack of leadership in an organisation, they would then leave because they did not see this as their problem.

Frameworks That Will Guide the Future

Often during the interviews, we realised that the discussion was not really about creating new leadership development ideas—rather, it was about positioning and implementing ideas, ideas that had been out for a while. These were positioned in the new world with more emphasis and urgency, and less of the claim to be right or to know it all and have found a fitting solution.

We summarise some of the main findings below (Fig. 4.1).

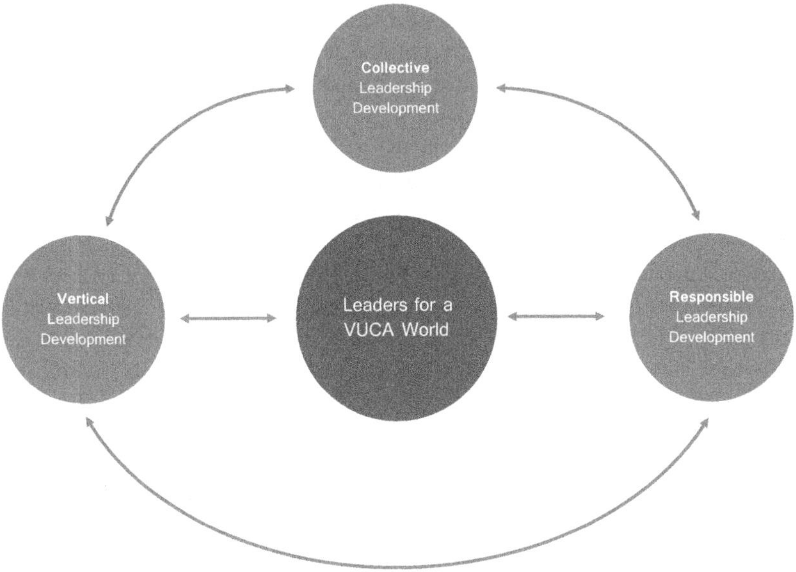

Fig. 4.1 Three key areas for leadership development to address as it moves forward. The areas are highly interconnected and often fluid

Responsible Leadership

In the section about the history of leadership development, we called responsible leadership the new kid on the block. This does not mean that it is a completely new concept—in fact, it is more of an umbrella embracing many other concepts in leadership development. This umbrella includes the concept of 'ethical leadership', which was often discussed at the beginning of the century, but never became a trend in leadership development. One reason for this might have been that some of its messages were rather patronising, utilising a moral mandate, which did not go down well with leaders who try to embrace many paradoxes within the main objective of making a positive difference and generating business.

In 2015, we ran a very successful leadership programme and invited leaders of charities to have a dialogue with the senior leaders of the corporation that the programme had been designed for. We also invited a speaker to talk about megatrends and innovation—all the leaders felt inspired by the exchange with leaders from completely different areas, reflecting together about the challenges of megatrends. The feedback was that they had learned a lot and as a result new thinking was triggered. Many of the ideas that they heard on the programme were probably not new to them, but they felt that the megatrend frameworks were useful to work with.

Just two years later, in 2017, we had a completely different experience and feedback, albeit in a similar setting. Some of the leaders expressed their frustration with the demand of the organisation to be the perfect, responsible and business-generating leader. They felt annoyance, mixed with some resignation. They felt that they knew the problems, and they even recognised that they were part of the problem, but were tired of being blamed. Their message was that they tried to act more ethically but they felt overwhelmed by the challenging work attitude of millennials and Gen Zs, as well as having more demanding clients. They argued that if they were not to focus on generating profit, then neither their organisation nor the economy in general could generate wealth for the population.

What had changed? We believe that in 2014/2015 the concept of responsible leadership was still new and theoretical, and so everybody liked the idea of being a good responsible leader. However, over the subsequent years, responsible leadership had become a must for any leader, and yet the business model of most organisations had not changed.

During the COVID-19 pandemic, people were scared, yet this was not reflected in comments from leaders who were creating even more insecurity. However, some leaders such as the German Chancellor Angela Merkel and the New Zealand Prime Minister Jacinda Ardern were praised for showing good examples of responsible leadership and communication during this period, giving the population confidence in the midst of a highly anxious period.

So how is it possible to integrate responsible leadership in leadership development? Over the last two decades, many leadership development interventions have been familiar and, as mentioned above, probably mainly take place at the first layer of leadership development—raising self-awareness and consciousness, and reflection on one's own values. Reflecting on one's own maturity as a leader is also very helpful to support leaders in their development (which will be further explored below on vertical leadership).

We found it extremely useful to invite leaders to reflect on and discuss different ethical dilemmas and/or paradoxes which they are confronted with in their roles as leaders—situations where there is no right or wrong, but a leadership decision needs to be made. What we were seeing was that a facilitated discussion with peers widened the leader's own perception, making them aware of their own unconscious biases and helping them embrace the complexity of a problem. There seems to also be a side effect that the leader's empathy and emotional intelligence are trained by accepting that they as leaders often face an ethical dilemma which has no right solution. Living and accepting uncertainty, and at the same time understanding the need to give guidance, are key for a responsible leader in a VUCA world.

We also asked participants to choose the values which were important for them in life and compare them with the company's values. Again, next to reflection, open and honest exchange with their peers was key to raising self-awareness and consciousness—but also being brave enough to take a decision without all the information, as well as on admitting failure if required.

And finally, we developed a small diagnostic on responsible leadership, asking leaders and students to judge themselves on their ability to:

- Make informed judgements;
- Show moral courage;
- Engage in strategic long-term thinking;
- Communicate effectively with key stakeholders;
- Participate in collective problem-solving.

For the senior leaders, as well as for our students, the most challenging aspect of responsible leadership was the last one—participating in collective problem-solving. Again and again, the same message came out—that the fifth layer of leadership development is the most demanding. The fifth layer is the one where individuals, teams and organisations struggle most, and this is also where we see countries struggling. Nevertheless, collective leadership is the level which will be key for sustainable political stability and economic growth, as the COVID-19 pandemic shows. We will explore this further in the following chapters.

Vertical Leadership Development

So, what is vertical leadership development? Horizontal development refers to the adding of more knowledge, skills, and competencies. Vertical development refers to advancement in a person's thinking capability. The outcome of vertical stage development is the ability to think in more complex, systemic, strategic, and interdependent ways (Petrie 2013).

Swiss psychologist, Jean Piaget, showed in a series of experiments that as children grow, the way they think advances through predictable stages. Piaget noticed that at each higher stage, children could think in more complex and sophisticated ways, meaning that they were able to deal with increasingly difficult problems.

Where Piaget left off in childhood, researchers like Robert Kegan (Kegan and Lahey 2009) and Bill Torbert (Rooke and Torbert 2005) picked up in adulthood. For a long time, it was assumed that once you reach adulthood, these stages of development would stop—after all, you are a grown-up, right? However, Kegan and others discovered that developmental stages do in fact continue into adulthood.

Why is vertical leadership development so important for the future? One answer is that, from a leadership perspective, researchers have shown that people at higher levels of development perform better in more complex environments. A study by Keith Eigel looked at 21 CEOs and 21 promising middle managers from various companies, each with annual revenues of over $5 billion. The study showed that across a range of leadership measures, there was a clear correlation between higher levels of vertical development and higher levels of effectiveness (Eigel and Kuhnert 2017).

In their highly accessible book on vertical development, *Upgrade*, Boston and Ellis use the analogy of a mobile phone. People can for a period of time keep adding more and more apps to their phones, but there comes a time when the operating system on the phone itself is unable to cope and hence the user needs to upgrade the device itself (Boston and Ellis 2019).

Another analogy might be the electrical wiring in your house. It works fine, but then you start to add more and more electrical gadgets in your kitchen and finally it blows—as one of the authors of this book discovered last Christmas!

Yes, we can help leaders develop by adding skills, such as how to give feedback, how to coach, how to influence, etc. However, to help leaders thrive in a world that is becoming increasingly complex, interconnected and unpredictable, we have to develop how they think.

So, what is the challenge for leadership developers? For all those involved in developing leaders, there will be a significant shift of role and, in turn, the mindset and skills needed to help leaders grow vertically.

Horizontal development is more about the transfer of expertise. Developers can draw upon their own knowledge bank and teach developing leaders the skills. There is a predictability and hence psychological safety in this approach. Both teacher and learner have a good sense of what to expect in the development process. It's a well-trodden path.

Vertical development requires that facilitators can, as Petrie (2013) describes it:

- Design heat experiences;
- Convene colliding perspectives;
- Facilitate elevated sense making.

These are designed to take leaders through three key stages that McGuire and Rhodes (2009) point to:

- Awaken;
- Unlearn;
- Advance.

Kegan deepens what is needed at each of these stages. In the awaken stage, people need to become frustrated by challenges, situations and dilemmas in their leadership work. In order to unlearn, they need space in which to test their old assumptions and try new ones. Finally, they need to have skilled support to help them persist, as they start to feel anxiety as they think and lead in the world through a new lens (Kegan and Lahey 2009).

For mentors, line managers and internal coaches, these are rarely the type of development experiences through which they themselves have built their skills. Most of their own experiences will have been characterised by horizontal development experiences. For the suppliers of leadership development, the capability to do this exists, although there are a number of barriers to the utilisation of these capabilities

Firstly, personal energy—the energy required from the learner and the facilitator—is so much higher when trying to grow vertically. It requires both parties to take themselves out of their comfort zones and consciously seek out 'heat experiences'. Petrie describes heat experiences as when,

> A leader faces a complex situation that disrupts and disorients his habitual way of thinking. He discovers that his current way of making sense of the world is inadequate. His mind starts to open and search for new and better ways to make sense of his challenge.

The energy required to do this is both mental and emotional. The thinking that is required to examine our own mental models of the world is often intense. The need to let go of a certain level of control can evoke fear, which is itself a particularly challenge form of emotional energy. As facilitators who have regularly worked in this territory, holding the space can in fact be exhausting. Often participants become anxious about where the development experience is taking them and as a result can lose trust in the facilitator. It requires a huge amount of emotional fortitude, not to mention confidence to hold your nerve and guide the participant through. Colleagues in the facilitation space have spoken to us about burnout and the need to strictly limit how much of this type of work they are doing.

Secondly, there is the issue of the economics of this type of development work. The ratios of facilitators to participants have to be low. This type of development does not fit well into large groups. Participants will react differently, needing personalised levels of support and challenge. This balance of support and challenge often has to be adjusted continually. Few clients in our experience are willing to fund this level of facilitation support. Where they are, the activity often has to be very focussed on leaders who they believe will have potential to reach higher levels in their organisation. In our experience, some companies are nervous about the message that this sends out to the wider organisation about how money is being spent on development.

On the supply side, vertical development is not easily sold as a scalable product, again due to the economics for the buyer. Taking this one layer down, suppliers recognise that the skills needed for this type of facilitation are sophisticated. Consultants therefore will be expensive and their potential margins are again challenged.

Lastly, measurement—buyers in organisations are naturally attracted to measuring the outcomes achieved by their development investments. Vertical development has always been significantly harder to measure than horizontal development. Observing people practising leadership behaviours in the territory of feedback giving, negotiation, handling conflict, etc., is feasible. Measuring how people are building thinking capabilities such as 'Perspective shifting, self-relating, opposable thinking and sense making' (Boston and Ellis 2019) is considerably harder. It can be done by observing over a period of time how leaders handle complex situations. However, again this is highly resource-intensive and does not fit well into the quantifiable scales that organisations like to use in their KPIs.

So, while these are the challenges to vertical development activity, there has never been a time when the need to help leaders grow in this area has been more acute. As we write these lines, leaders across the world are grappling with the COVID-19 pandemic. It would be hard to argue that this is not an extraordinary and alarming reinforcement of the VUCA world, through which leaders have to navigate.

Building Collective Leadership

The challenges our society faces are highly complex and beyond the capability of any single leader to solve. Leadership input from a wide and diverse range of stakeholders is needed to make sense of what is required to move forward.

So, why is building collective leadership which takes mainly place on the fifth layer of leadership development so critical to the future of our world?

While we were in the middle of writing this book, the COVID-19 pandemic broke out. We had started this chapter at the beginning of January 2020, discussing the need for collective leadership to tackle climate change. However, even at the beginning of 2020, we were aware that unfortunately, this was not a main priority for many people. Then, COVID-19 shocked the world. No country can look away anymore or build walls to protect themselves. Suddenly, collective leadership became a must—exchange of knowledge benefits everybody. Supporting less-wealthy countries became self-interest, as, for example, setting up a global vaccine fund and building a support net for developing countries were no longer just a 'nice-to-have'. Global leadership, collective leadership, means protecting us and especially the vulnerable all over the world. International agreements—even rules on hygiene—became a must to guarantee our global health. Collective leadership is a must.

In the light of this, how can we build collective leadership and how can we include this in leadership development? Snowden in his Cynefin framework (Snowden 1999) describes the need for leaders to recognise complex situations where a very different response is required. In contrast to simple leadership challenges which were previously solved and best practice could simply be followed, or complicated problems which could be solved by the brightest people. Instead, for complex leadership challenges, the 'right solution' does not exist. Instead, it will simply be the best solution at that point in time with the knowledge currently available. This again can only be done by collective leadership, by bringing a diverse team of leaders together and by listening to different knowledge, perspectives and experiences before taking a decision.

Building these sorts of capabilities in leaders is very different from the way it has been done in the past. The old model of leadership development was that well-established, in a sense proven, competencies could be developed in individual leaders (see Chapter 2). These enhanced capabilities, once built into development workshops, could then be transferred back into the organisational setting as leaders came back together.

However, often this did not work, as leaders tried to behave differently within a system which had not changed. Other people in the system would push back against the efforts of the recently developed leader to try something new. While the old leader they knew was certainly not perfect, they preferred the predictability that the old state provided. Virginia Satir, in her pioneering work on family systems therapy, points to the need to work with the whole system in developing new behaviours. The system in her particular focus was the family. The 'problem child' was part of a wider system that was sustaining the behavioural pattern.

Much is talked about and many efforts are made to maximise the transfer of learning back into the workplace. Learning and development professionals recognise the importance of line managers following up and reinforcing new learning. Unfortunately, despite these well-intentioned efforts, it can often be the line managers' behaviours that are getting in the way of change.

How can systems of leaders grow together to build sustainable change? This question is becoming an even more important one, as what is meant by the system becomes much wider. Before organisational boundaries were well defined, organisational charts provided a sense of how it all worked. Now collaborative working across a multitude of partners means that some partners are employed by the host organisation, some are self-employed, some are suppliers, and some are customers.

At a recent public sector team leadership development session, one participant asked why the supplier was not in the room, as they felt that it was their behaviours that were the most significant in preventing change. The response from the senior leader in the room was that this team needed to form and establish its position before opening the doors to other stakeholders. An understandable position, but one that potentially slowed down or even blocked the development of collective leadership on the project, because the work of forming would effectively needed to be begun again when the suppliers join the group. Worse still, the suppliers would potentially come with resistance and may be even suspicion, driven by their lack of early inclusion.

Building collective leadership requires individuals within sponsoring organisations to let go of the need for control. Bringing together a wide range of people from different organisations is often a significant step into the unknown.

One of our clients recently brought together 150 leaders from a huge variety of organisations to tackle large societal challenges, while building the collective leadership capability to tackle other significant problems. An outstanding leader that we have had the privilege to work with for many years. He knew that the first job was to find a question that would inspire them to come together. Finding the convening question that would inspire their sustained attendance took many days of refinement.

The second job was to build enough trust in the room that the conversation could start in a way that was generative and expansive, as opposed to the jockeying for position that characterises many early stages of people coming together for the first time.

The convening leader expressed to us his nervousness about the event. He felt that showing up with a question to inspire and an intention to build trust was not enough preparation. We talked and helped him see that his job as the leader was to hold the space long enough so that others would step up and lead with him for the whole.

Collective change and leadership growth happen when leaders can create the space where different patterns of conversation can emerge. This takes courage, as structure and process, and ultimately control, have to take a back seat.

Tools to Get There

During our interviews, leadership development tools repeatedly surfaced which seemed to be successful time and again, over many years. Even more so, these tools were safe and reliable and will remain so for the foreseeable future. The following graphic gives an overview of these interventions (Fig. 4.2).

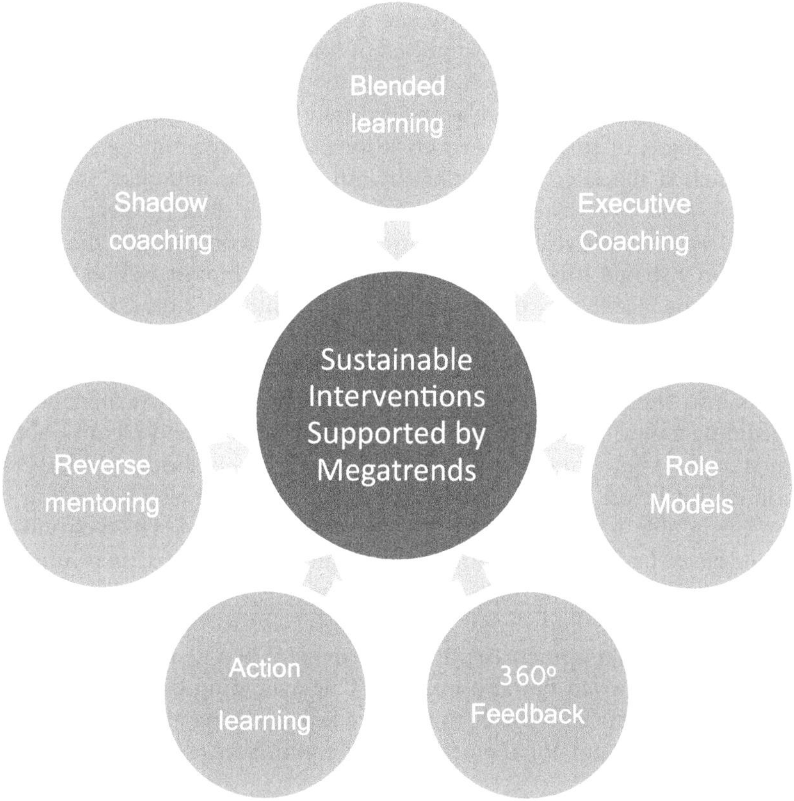

Fig. 4.2 Forms of leadership development which we suggest will endure into the future

Role Models

The idea of learning from role models is not a new one in leadership development, and it is a common practice to invite senior leaders to leadership development events to share their experience. To make it more personal, we ask the leaders to think of challenging times when they have felt very vulnerable and/or to think about something they are really proud of.

During one of our leadership development modules for new partners in a professional service firm, we saw both good examples of how role modelling works and also illustrations of how it fails.

The first senior leader started talking about a skiing trip where he and his group went off-piste and were surprised by an avalanche. He shared the challenges of this situation, his fears and how relieved he felt when they reached the safety of the ski hut. All along the audience, including the facilitator, were listening rather stunned. They didn't expect a 'hero' story they couldn't really connect to, and were wondering if the senior leader only shared this tale because it still showed him in a good light.

The other leader started completely differently by first asking everybody what they were worrying about. Not surprisingly, they felt the pressure to generate new business, motivate the team and integrate themselves into the firm's leadership team. He then shared his experience of becoming a new partner in the firm in IT, just before the dot.com bubble burst at the beginning of this century. He shared his shock, his desperation of not being able to create income, his fears and also his feeling of not being able to deliver what was expected from him. He then talked about his difficult path to refocus, cooperate with other partners and the hard task in developing skills in an area he wasn't an expert in—in his case to deepen his knowledge in financial service to be able to generate business and build up new client relationships. When he finished, the new partners were moved but also inspired. Understanding that both cooperation and humility in difficult times were key for being able to 'stand up' again was important for them, and they could connect to him as a real role model.

So, what is a role model? According to the Oxford English Dictionary, a role model is a person who serves as an example of the values, attitudes and behaviours associated with a role.

The senior leader in our second example did exactly this. The value of cooperation, his attitude to move on and create something new, and on the behavioural side his resilience and endurance, was exactly the spirit the professional service firm wanted to be seen by the new leaders, and it was great that he contributed to this leadership development event. Yet he did even more than this—he actively listened to the young partners' concerns, building up a rapport with them by being authentic and emotionally intelligent.

Reflecting on the key theme of this book, we also discussed with our students and our interviewees the importance of role models in times of megatrends. Several of the leadership development suppliers, as well as the HR professionals, felt that while the need and wish to have role models are inherent in human beings, there was a lack of role model leaders. They shared their experience that in many organisations the senior leaders are often not seen as role models because they appear not to show what is expected by a role model.

Students and HR professionals stated that, from a millennial perspective, current leaders are often living a life which they do not desire. One HR professional, a millennial herself, described the example of a leader who starts reading his emails while brushing his teeth in the morning and finishes working late in the night, still sending final emails. What might have been seen 20 years ago as 'role modelling behaviour' demonstrating high commitment and dedication to the work is now seen by his team as worrying and a life that they do not aspire to. This might explain the high number of young employees leaving the firm after three to four years—exactly the time when they have become well trained and have reached the managerial level to take over leadership responsibilities.

On the student side, it was also expressed that some of the megatrends such as disparity of wealth and climate change were in fact created by the previous generation, but now they do not show 'role model' behaviour in tackling these challenges. Sharing this feedback to senior leaders, some of them could connect to it, although they always expressed that they felt overwhelmed themselves and did not know how to act as a 'role model' when facing megatrends.

Aligned with this, one leadership development supplier reflected that while the desire for role models was probably more imminent than ever, it caused leaders to look backwards. He emphasised that the focus on what leaders have learned in the past and seen with other leaders in the past is not what leadership means for tomorrow.

The same problem has been acknowledged for many years when looking at the most favourite teaching tools used at business school—case studies. Case studies, books which were seen as the 'best in class', and leaders as 'the role models' for the future all prove to be unsustainable. As previously mentioned, famous for his glorified leader role model was Fred Goodwin who was once cited as an example of how to build collaborative teams, due to the way he had quickly integrated the acquisition of NatWest with RBS. Less than a year later, during the onset of the financial crisis, he was accused of huge levels of arrogance and an unwillingness to listen to dissenting voices. In 2010, he drove RBS into complete crisis.

However, many others struggle to maintain the status of role model in the face of megatrends. Take Richard Branson, who is certainly adored by many and always mentioned as a role model—even when we asked students to think about leader role models four years ago he was still named. Today, due to climate change, the airline industry is being questioned. Even more so, Branson's recent announcement that he wants to open a cruise business, one of the most polluting businesses within the tourism sector, demonstrates how accepted role models in leadership do not seem to be able to handle all the challenges of the megatrends.

The example of Richard Branson illustrates that simply repeating what used to work in the past is not enough to face the complexity of megatrends. Climate change data has been around for a long time, but now society is catching up with what it actually means. Although there is usually a time delay, societal values eventually catch up with technology and scientific information.

In summary, to meet the challenge of being a role model in times of megatrends, we believe that it is helpful to apply the five layers of leadership development. It has been repeated again and again that role modelling on the first three layers was something which traditionally worked well. Yet the real challenge for role models takes place on layers four and five—simply because there are no leaders around who have successfully and sustainably shown how to make it work.

Coaching

As previously mentioned, coaching (or more specifically, executive coaching) has become a safe place for leaders to develop. It has also become a safe place where HR professionals can address individual development issues in a very targeted, as well as confidential, way. One-to-one coaching is a preferred leadership development intervention on the first layer of leadership development, as it mainly begins with the leaders themselves and their respective current leadership challenges. It also occurs on the second layer of leadership development by using the coach as a sounding board about how to improve the team effectiveness. However, this is not where coaching should end. The coach should be a useful sparring partner for the third, fourth and fifth layers of leadership development—examples being how to change the culture of their organisation, what kind of leadership the profession needs, and how the leader themselves and their organisation can contribute to solving the fifth layer challenges (such as the plastic war, rise in mental health issues, handling a pandemic and being prepared for similar future events).

In general, it can be stated that over the last 20 years executive coaching has come a long way. From being an intervention for the 'difficult but high-potential' employees, or sometimes the 'difficult but cannot be fired' personnel, it has now become a well-established leadership tool which seems to go from strength to strength. With a slow start at the beginning of the last century, the amount of literature and research now in existence about coaching demonstrates that it has become an established leadership development intervention.

So, why did this happen? Research shows that the brain produces dopamine when an individual talks about oneself, which might be one of the reasons for the success of coaching. Or, as one coachee once expressed it, 'Having coaching is like going to the movies – but I am the main character'. However, this is just a part of the answer—in the leadership development world the demand for coaching is well aligned with at least four major trends (Fig. 4.3).

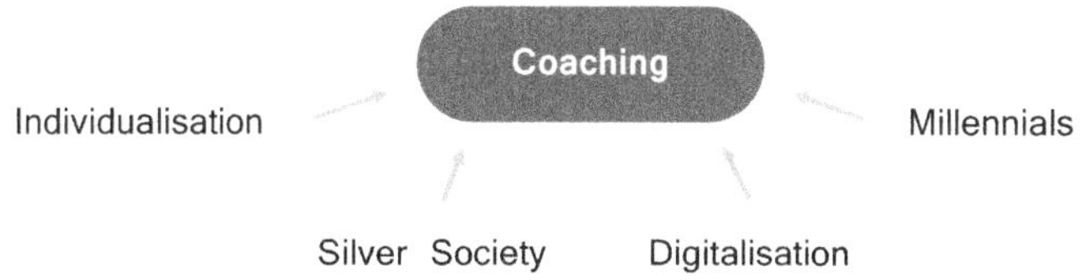

Fig. 4.3 How well coaching is suited as a form of leadership development to match the changes in behaviour triggered by megatrends

The first seems to be **individualisation**. From water bottles with our name engraved on them, to receiving tailor-made adverts after surfing the Internet for certain products, people have become used to a world around them which meets their own individual needs. This wish for personalised products and services works very much in favour of one-to-one coaching. Here is the executive coach, usually trying to fit into the busy world of a leader, who listens to the leader's stories, dreams, fears and frustrations, and then helps them to move on, to become more resilient. If the coach is psychologically trained, they can often help discover and reduce limiting beliefs, unhelpful auto-pilots or even mini-traumata. So an attractive leadership development tool for a VUCA world where simple solutions no longer exist.

Along with the trend for individualisation comes the fact that potential coaches, especially at a more senior level, expect the coach to fit into their time schedule and ideally come to where they are located. This places on the supplier a demand for a higher grade of flexibility, or for more coaches to be available.

This need for flexibility helps the second trend, the rise of coaches coming from the **'silver society'**—baby-boomers and Gen-X coaches who are semi-retired and are entering the coaching market in their second career.

In addition, coaching fits well into a third major trend—that of **remote working**. Since the COVID-19 outbreak, remote working has become key for our society. Due to the technological advancements that facilitate office-free collaboration with video-conferencing, suppliers have established stable platforms for interacting virtually. Out of all leadership development interventions, one-to-one coaching seems to be the obvious choice which works well remotely, while still being connected.

Both authors have worked virtually with their coachees for many years, with positive results. However, based on our experiences, a mix between face-to-face sessions and remote coaching often works best.

Besides the logistical advantages of coaching as a leadership development tool, the fourth major trend which influences the success story of coaching is the **expectations of millennials** and Gen Z. When we asked our MBA students (who were mainly millennials) what characteristics a leader should have, authenticity and emotional intelligence were two of the attributes which were mentioned. Furthermore, in a study run by one of the authors and a millennial student about what millennials expect at their workplace, the majority reported that being coached was key for them to stay with their employer (Hieker 2019).

So, out of all leadership development interventions, it's no surprise that coaching is probably the one which has continuously grown and will continue to do so.

With the rise of coaching, the idea of 'leader as a coach' (Peterson et al. 1996), established for the first time at the end of the last century, is now an accepted concept. Despite the conflict leaders might often feel between their role as line managers and their role as a coach, it is expected that leaders are competent coaches as well as being able to actively listen, give constructive feedback and be emotionally intelligent.

As a consequence, organisations are keen to support leaders in acquiring the needed coaching skills. Coaching skills training for leaders is a widely accepted leadership development intervention, which began at the start of this century. Both authors have run many of these trainings in the last decade, as many organisations felt this offered a quick win to change the leaders' skills and behaviour. Implicitly, there is also the hope that the roll-out of coaching skill training will eventually have an effect on the culture of an organisation, influencing its metamorphosis into a coaching culture.

While the expectation that leaders should be able to act as a coach, the leadership development interventions that support this have changed during this past decade—for a couple of reasons. Firstly, training budgets were reduced and classroom training was diminished, and secondly, due to the megatrend of digitisation, any kind of 'how to coach' training is now available online and offered by many global companies.

However, one major outcome of the interviews, as well as the authors' own observations, is that the ability of a leader to coach is now something that is widely expected. It has become almost a basic skill, in the same way that the ability to be a good presenter (for example) is expected. Companies no longer feel the need and obligation to offer this training, as they feel that any leader should be able to do it.

However, most of the time, the reality is that this is not the case, and the gap between reality and expectations becomes larger than ever. This leads to another trend in the leadership development arena—the development of internal coaches.

Internal Coaches and Mentors
In addition to the skill gap mentioned, many line managers feel that there is an inherent conflict in the different roles they are being asked to play—line managing people in terms of appraisal and pay, while trying to create a safe environment in which their employees can be vulnerable and coachable. The response has been an investment in building internal coaches and mentors.

The authors have worked for many organisations—especially in banking and professional service firms—that train 'internal coaches' who are available for more junior employees where external coaching would be too expensive. Another example is an initiative of one major retail organisation to offer internal coaching for all senior employees so that they can then 'coach' somebody more junior in another division.

Mentoring done well needs to be underpinned by strong coaching skills, and this has also formed part of internal training offering

Coaching can become a key part of changing an organisation's culture—facilitating conversations about coaching mindset, coaching approach and coaching leadership style. Observing the increasing need in coaching skills at all hierarchy levels, it is surprising that acquiring coaching skills is still something which mainly happens when you are already a leader in an organisation—or, as mentioned above, you might be sent for a time-consuming coaching training, mostly in the later stage of your career.

Like presentation skills and, hopefully, basic communication and team skills, coaching should be a key part of any curriculum at universities, as it is almost too late to learn them when you actually need to use them.

In summary, the strong influence of the concept of coaching on all different levels of an organisation might almost be considered a megatrend in the leadership development arena in itself—something which has changed and will continue to change the leadership development landscape.

Shadow Coaching

Even though the name gives it away and 'shadow coaching' is often seen as a product which is offered by leadership development suppliers in the context of coaching, we decided to position it as a separate leadership development intervention, between coaching and action learning.

many of the existing mental models that leaders carry are outdated. Action learning provides a powerful methodology to help leaders see this for themselves, while working through very practical challenges.

The penultimate idea is that many leaders attending development workshops are concerned about the time away from 'real work' that it requires. The way in which action learning tackles live challenges provides leaders with immediate practical takeaways representing a strong ROI on their valuable time. This is very different from leaders reviewing historical case studies, which they often find hard to relate back to current situations.

Lastly, once established, such action learning groups can work in a virtual setting supported by the technology now available. This is beneficial as it supports organisations' increasing commitment to reduce their carbon footprint in relation to travel. Working in such a way is also appealing to millennials' working preferences.

Action learning in our experience needs skilled facilitation to establish this approach to learning. It is, however, a set of facilitation skills that can be gradually learnt by the group members themselves. This makes it appealing to organisations as they wish to build their internal capabilities as opposed to relying on external consultants and coaches.

The Power of 360-Degree Feedback

360-degree feedback has now been seen for decades as a very powerful tool to support a leader in his/her development. Most companies develop their own in-house 360-degree feedback (or sometimes just 180-degree feedback).

Especially during the last three to five years, with some of our clients we have seen that they have included the idea of vertical leadership in their 360-degree feedback. Realising that the maturity of a leader is not judged by numbers and P&L, they aligned their questionnaires to some of the key ideas described above in the section on vertical leadership development as well as the section on responsible leadership.

While standardised questionnaires often have little added value in information terms for the receiver of the feedback, the answers to qualitative questions are often very insightful. Even in standardised questionnaires, the so-called annex about 'should continue doing', 'should stop doing', 'should start doing', usually brings more insights than simply marking numbers.

Potential questions for qualitative 360-degree feedback could include:

- When this person is at his/her best as a leader, what do they bring to the organisation/team and conversation?
- Where does this person need to grow as a leader to meet the challenges of the future?
- What does this person need to watch out for in the way that they lead?
- What three words would you use to describe this person as a leader?
- If you were this person's leadership coach, what would you say to them?

However, to make the 360-degree feedback even leaner, the questions might even be reduced to:

- When this person is at his/her best as a leader, what do they bring to the organisation/team and conversation?
- Where does this person need to grow as a leader to meet the challenges of the future?
- What three words would you use to describe this person as a leader?

Our experience shows that the 'three attributes' feedback question in particular is much appreciated by the person receiving feedback. It offers something tangible to remember and take away.

On other occasions, we have run 360-degree feedback interviews which were usually not longer than 20 minutes and simply asked the interviewee:

- what the person was good at;
- where he/she should develop;
- any recommendations.

Running an interview in this unstructured (phenomenological) way is much more work for the leadership development supplier, as he/she has to bring structure, cluster information together and find the appropriate headings. Another challenge for the person who runs the 360-degree feedback is to find the right balance of keeping the original feedback of the 360-degree feedback nominees, and at the same time making sure that the feedback is anonymised.

In general, we believe that this is one of the most powerful tools in leadership development, as it is a unique chance for the feedback receiver to understand how he/she is perceived by different peers. In our experience, an interview-based feedback is usually more honest than written feedback. The way in which interviewees prioritise their answers may already provide valuable insight. Usually, the most dominant characteristic of a person is positioned first. Even when we begin an interview by inviting the feedback giver to talk about strengths first, most feedback givers would bring up their main concerns before even being asked.

Reverse Mentoring

Many senior executives have shared with us over the years that they often feel overwhelmed by the speed of technology advancement, and even more so that they as leaders should lead to this change. This concern was even expressed by senior leaders in technology companies, as well as leaders who were responsible for the technology departments in banks and industry. One of the most difficult challenges they faced was the feeling some of the questions they wished to ask were potentially so basic that it would be embarrassing.

At the same time, millennials felt that leadership development is often isolated from real-world challenges, even though they like to have impact in the workplace (Barrington and Luetchford 2019). In an attempt to meet these different needs of two generations, a new leadership development intervention has quietly taken place in organisations during the last 5–10 years, called 'reverse mentoring'.

Based on the idea of a mentor being someone who is more experienced and usually at a more senior level in an organisation, to accelerate a junior employee's development reverse mentoring (or upward mentoring) aims to equip senior leaders with the knowledge and language to operate in the digital world (Microsoft News Centre Europe 2018).

While it started rather informally when senior leaders reached out to young talented IT specialists to talk about different technical topics, reverse mentoring is now introduced by many HR departments as a formal development offer. Interested senior leaders are matched with a millennial or even Gen Z employees who often work in the IT department of the firm.

During the interview process, one of the senior leaders explained how helpful he found the interaction with his reverse mentor, and that for him, next to coaching, this was the leadership development tool he benefited most from. He met his 'junior mentor' twice monthly and the sessions usually were 30 minutes to an hour long. His tip was to make the most out of it by preparing the sessions. He made it a habit to collect questions, expressions and abbreviations that he doesn't feel familiar with during his working day. He can then ask all the 'stupid' questions of his reverse mentor when they meet. Having done this for more than six months, he now felt much better equipped as head of operations to run his unit. He was also very clear that he wanted to continue the interaction with his 'IT mentor'. He mentioned that he liked the interaction and discussion with the new generation where he often received more honest feedback than he would usually as a senior leader in an organisation. We also liked that he admitted that he cringed when his young mentor pitifully looked at him during their first meeting, commenting that it must be hard learning this in a later age rather than being a 'digital native'.

Reflecting on some of the megatrends we have discussed, it is no surprise that reverse mentoring has become very successful. The obvious trend this relates to is digitisation, but the trend of individualisation can also be seen here again—senior leaders asking their own individual questions and receiving special attention. In addition, as mentioned above, the millennial generation also receives attention and feels that they bring value to the workplace, something which is important to them.

As discussed in the coaching section, it is also important to reflect on how to best develop these mentors. For senior mentors, it is now fairly common to offer mentor training/supervision, especially when they are supporting, for example, the participant of a high-potential programme. However, not much is done at the moment to support this generation of 'reverse mentors'. Surely, as reverse mentoring becomes an established tool, training will also be offered for the junior mentors. It would be an interesting experiment to bring both groups of mentors together to discuss the challenge of mentoring. None of the HR professionals we spoke to had run a similar intervention, but some were very interested in what this would mean for the culture of an organisation.

Developing Leaders Who Can Meet the Challenges of Mental Health

The World Health Organisation claims that depression and anxiety have a significant economic impact; the estimated cost to the global economy is US$1 trillion per year in lost productivity. Globally, an estimated 264 million people suffer from depression, one of the leading causes of disability, with many of these people also suffering from symptoms of anxiety (WHO 2019).

Data from other sources reinforces the point. A Lancet Commission report highlighted that mental disorders are rising around the world and will cost the global economy $16 trillion by 2030. An estimated 12 billion working days are lost due to mental illness every year.

Evidence in the UK from the Mental Health Organisation suggests that 12.7% of all sickness absence days can be attributed to mental health conditions, such as stress, depression and anxiety.

The National Institute of Mental Health highlights that the leading cause of absence in the USA is depression, and figures from the World Health Organization (WHO) suggest that in many developed countries between 35 and 45% of work absences can be attributed to mental health problems (WHO 2019).

These statistics suggest that how organisations work with mental health challenges will have a huge impact on their overall effectiveness. Leaders have a large part to play in building environments which support people struggling with their mental health, as well as not creating a work culture which pushes people into this place.

Helping senior leaders develop the mindset that they as role models have a significant part to play in leading mental health issues is challenging. Many leaders have their own insecurities, the often cited 'imposter syndrome' (Clance and Imes 1978) being one of them. These insecurities are often worked through in the relatively safe space of personal coaching. However, to really lead others in this space, they need to be willing and confident to do more. Many leaders who are towards the top of their organisational hierarchies developed at time when awareness of mental health challenges was far less commonplace. Back then, displaying the personal vulnerability needed to convene such a conversation in the workplace was seen as weak.

In our experience, the first step is to create psychologically safe spaces, often in small groups of peers, where their own experiences of mental health challenges can be shared. Many leaders that we have worked with are often relieved—and to some extent energised—to realise that they were not alone in having some of these challenges. This often then provides a platform from which to work more proactively with their wider organisations.

However, there are significant questions around the legitimacy organisations have to ask leaders to explore this territory in development settings. We as authors have experienced workshops where participants have formally complained to their organisations about being asked to work in this territory.

The second challenge is around whether facilitators have the right background and qualifications to take leaders into this territory. Clearly, leadership development work often creates environments and conversations where personal disclosure may occur. However, explicitly asking leaders to explore these types of issues sharpens these questions of capability.

Culture also plays a significant role here. Certain sectors, such as investment banking or the legal profession, may be more resistant to this type of leadership development work, whereas charitable organisations may be more predisposed. The layer of national culture could also be added to this mix. Certain parts of the world, such as the USA, have embraced the role of counselling in mainstream life longer than most.

The choice of leadership development channels utilised to work in this area also needs to be thought through. One-to-one coaching may well be very suited, as it is a closed environment where boundaries of confidentiality are generally well observed. Small group action learning can also work well. The relatively expensive cost per head of these channels means that it is often more senior leaders who benefit from them. However, there are many leaders lower down organisations that are often at the sharp end of dealing with mental health challenges in their teams. Useful guidelines can be provided in e-learning formats, but often of course do not create the open exchange that is so often useful in exploring a very nuanced area of leadership development.

Another question that organisations are also grappling with, given the questions of boundaries and capability, is to what extent this is a role for mainstream leaders. Some organisations are providing more specialised training to people within HR teams. Others may feel that this is a specialised function that can be outsourced. While this approach is understandable, leaders still need to be able to spot the signs effectively and early enough so that useful referrals can be made. Mainstream leaders also still have the role of creating cultures in which people struggling would contact the relevant specialists, secure in the belief that it would not be held against them. (See the story above about the role of one of the authors as a specialist psychologist in a business intervention.)

The current situation with the COVID-19 pandemic is throwing up a fresh challenge for leaders. How do they stay in touch with their employee's mental health while working remotely? While this is accentuated during the isolation of a pandemic, more and more leaders are working with the challenge of teams that are dispersed across different geographies. For many people who already struggle with mental health issues, being isolated worsens their personal situation. For those that are prone to mental health issues, it can be a trigger point. Talking to leaders during the pandemic, we realised that they found it very challenging to keep engagement high while using virtual technologies. Most recognised the need for increasing the amount of connection with regular catch-ups with their teams. However, how to do it skilfully in a virtual context is clearly something that many were unprepared for. Some asked for facilitation support in this space. The learning curve for both leaders and suppliers of leadership development is currently a steep one.

Parts of the supply side of the industry have of course responded. Large numbers of articles and reports have been published online as to how to build your resilience during such a crisis. Apps, which support people in the mental health space, have come to the fore. Mental health at work, campaigners have welcomed this opportunity to raise the profile of the challenge. Many organisations, such as Procter and Gamble, have long been training their leaders in mindfulness techniques. Perhaps the COVID-19 situation will encourage a broader span of organisations to do more in helping leaders work with mental health challenges.

We are conscious in this piece that we are raising more questions than answers in the leadership development space. We do know from our experience of designing workshops in partnership with clients that more attention could be given to this area. Very infrequently would a client overtly and proactively ask for this to be included in the content. We may have already touched on many of the reasons for this, and we do acknowledge that sometimes requests are made using different language, for example, 'building resilience'. Perhaps it is time for clients and suppliers of leadership development interventions to have more overt and specific conversations about the challenges of mental health.

Leadership Development Channels

In the light of the megatrends previously explored, this chapter will explore the question of which channels are likely to be effective for the leadership development work of the future. In using the word 'channels', we mean the form of delivery—for example, lecture-based, e-learning, one-to-one coaching, action learning, etc.

As an anchor point for the discussion, we would like to use the learning cycle described by Kolb (1984). Kolb views learning as an integrated process. He believes that there are four stages that are essential to effective learning. The four stages he describes are Experience, Reflection, Conceptualise and Test. Each of the stages is mutually supportive of the others and feeds into the next. While he believes that it is possible to enter the cycle at any stage, to build effective learning we need to follow the logical sequence and complete all four stages.

Leadership development design for the future needs to ensure that participants are given the opportunity to go through all four stages. Ultimately, this means that some channels of development such as coaching and action learning need to be combined with the opportunity to try out the ideas explored. Strong executive coaches will often set clients assignments in line with this.

Certain parts of the learning cycle are challenging and yet crucial for leadership development in the future. In our experience, building reflective practices with participants is demanding. Leaders are often being bombarded with distractions, mainly in the flood of different forms of digitally fed information constantly coming at them. Smartphone addiction and the ways in which this can interrupt such a reflective space are an obvious example. We have been part of many design conversations around leadership development workshops about how to keep participants off their mobiles. Pushing back against this pervasive habit is hard.

One memorable example of this was a carefully designed leadership development intervention we participated in near Mexico City. On the second day of the workshop, a group of 30 leaders gathered before sunrise near some beautiful pyramids just outside the city. Blank notebooks were distributed to participants and a reflective question was posed: 'What sort of leadership does your organisation need to flourish into the future?' The leaders were then asked to find a quiet space on their own near the pyramids as the sun was rising, to reflect on this question. The time allocated was half-an-hour. Within minutes, phones were out and emails were being checked! Obviously, this was not helpful for deeper reflection, and it showed even more that helping leaders build structured reflective practices is crucial.

Another part of Kolb's learning cycle is the conceptualise step. Another way of viewing this is thinking about how we frame our experiences and reflections using theory. A huge source for this theory is the books and other materials that leaders read, watch and listen to. A number of renowned leaders, such as Bill Gates and Warren Buffett, are famous for the amount they read every day. Gates often attributes his success as a leader to his reading habits. The challenge though for leadership development within this is how to help leaders choose the material which they consume.

We often start live workshops by asking leaders how many books they believe have been written on the subject of leadership. This is intended as a playful, engaging question, but with a serious message behind it. The answer is clearly huge, and there is little point in trying to find the exact number. We are often asked by clients to recommend material to read, and given that we have explored a lot of material over the years, we can make a helpful contribution to this. However, in a world where many of the challenges are complex, ensuring that a leader is exposed to a wide range of perspectives through which to work on these challenges is crucial. It is important to acknowledge to ourselves as developers that our advice on what leaders should read will come from a limited perspective and value-based system. We as facilitators of leadership development will naturally have a view on what good leadership is and is not.

We wrote this chapter during the 'lockdown' needed in response to the global threat presented by COVID-19. During this time, significant parts of human development moved into the virtual world. Clients asked us what our online offering looked like, and at university, we suddenly had to offer our lectures in a virtual form.

However, there are very real challenges within this. A huge amount of leadership development happens through conversation between learners. How this can be facilitated virtually requires thought. The type of generative conversations that evolve in groups where non-verbal cues, such as body language and collective energy, are crucial and will be hard to replicate online. People's capacity to stay with this concentration for longer periods online is also questionable. Prior to the lockdown, we ran a team-based workshop where two of the team were unable to attend. The workshop was an intense event spanning two days. Feedback during the workshop and at the end was that this was extremely tiring for those physically not present in the physical room with other group members. We, as facilitators, have also attempted to do extended sessions online and have found it exhausting.

At many business schools, students push back against starting in a virtual form. A key reason that they have cited is the need to establish new relationships in a face-to-face manner. We know from previous experience that one of the key reasons that participants sign up for MBA programmes is the quality of the network they hope to build for the future with other participants. An assumption which everybody made became very clear during the COVID-19 crises. MBA students of leading business schools signed a petition that they would not accept the change to online classes because they felt that this would not give them the same learning experience (Moules 2020).

In other chapters of this book, we have spoken of the importance of vertical development and collective leadership development for leading in future. Certain channels of leadership development are better suited to growing leaders in this way. Vertical development requires that leaders are exposed to 'heat experiences'—these are essentially providing leaders with experiences that disorientate them and push them to challenge their existing assumptions about the world. It is hard to picture that online learning platforms would create this type of experience. Generally, these will need to be very carefully designed workshop experiences where complex challenges are given to groups of leaders who then need to make sense of them collectively. One research interviewee recalled a hugely powerful and memorable business simulation that she had been part of as an example of this type of development. Other channels of development, which are likely to be effective in this space, are stretching work-based assignments with coaching and action learning-based sense making structured around them.

Many organisations, both private and public, have invested heavily in physical centres where employees attend leadership development workshops. Examples of this are Crotonville (General Electric), Four Acres (Unilever) and Sandhurst (UK military). These centres have become symbols of the importance that the organisations place upon development. At one level, they would appear to be an expensive overhead that may drive organisations to design workshops around their existence to use available capacity. At another level, organisations cite these places as being crucial in building cultural norms as leaders gather at these centres.

At the heart of developing leaders' ability to lead collectively across systems and boundaries is a need to grow their relationship building capability. For many years, Unilever would consciously cultivate this capability through its workshops at the aforementioned Four Acres centre in southwest London. Huge levels of social capital were created through the networks built here, stretching right across the Unilever world. This type of investment in leadership support networks will be crucial for the future.

Organisations are now encouraging employees at all levels to demonstrate leadership. The idea that leadership is the responsibility of a select group towards the top of the organisational hierarchy is becoming outdated, and for good reason. The VUCA nature of the world means that often employees need to step out of defined process and bring leadership. Many channels of leadership development can be expensive and therefore hard to give access to across all these organisational levels. A clear response to this has been Massive Open Online Courses (MOOCs). This has provided a platform through which many traditional leadership development suppliers, such as Harvard Business School, have provided relatively inexpensive access to development. Undoubtedly, for people who are highly motivated to grow their leadership skills, this is a hugely important positive step.

However, there are a number of challenges that are associated with the MOOCs channel. Completion rates are proving to be low—15% is the highest estimate we found. It also relies on user-created content which can generate a potentially chaotic learning environment.

In general, we can clearly see that soft skills, including communication skills, active listening and giving feedback—which are basic but nevertheless key in being a good leader—can be delivered online as a way to understand the concepts and aid practice. In addition, role-plays, understanding others' facial expressions and their emotion will be something which will be delivered more and more via sophisticated online learning programme.

We also know from our own experience that one-to-one coaching works best with more sophisticated platforms where screens and/or whiteboards can be shared. Having the opportunity to share video seems to help many coaches that we have talked to. However, many coaches we asked explained that doing this electronically is sometimes even more exhausting than doing it in person, which might be due to the fact that the sender's audio and video do not always reach the receiver at the same time and therefore the receiver is constantly trying to accommodate to this time delay. This makes the task more challenging for both coach and coachee to understand the whole picture using their head, heart and gut to let the message sink in.

Having had many 'deep dives' in online one-to-one coachings, we know that it is not limited to 'transactional' coaching such as building up one's own network, agreeing on goals and action steps. It can also give opportunity for transformational coaching. We often find it helpful to use models such as the 'immunity to change' (Kegan and Lahey 2009), or at the end of a coaching journey a half-standardised reflection on 'goals achieved and things to be proud of' to take place during an online coaching session. Here, the coach can type up the coachee's reflection and so the coachee can keep this as a 'takeaway'. However, most of the coaches and coachees we asked about their preference felt that a mix of online and face to face was ideal. Online coaching can reduce travel time, increase flexibility and often offer 'just-in-time' coaching, but on other occasions the 'touch and feel' of being in the same room is preferable, especially if tools such as the empty chair work from Gestalt are used.

What we learned at the time of the COVID-19 pandemic, when all leadership development was digital, was that in a larger group setting, the danger of moving from contributor to consumer is much higher than in face-to-face settings. Well thought through breakout groups with clear instructions, short periods for reflection and then exchange of findings in the 'main' room are key to keeping attention of the participants. Role-plays, where two participants would play out a difficult situation with just their screens switched on, can also work, especially in a more 'training' MBA setting.

However, when asked, 'How is leadership training best provided?' the millennials in our research gave the highest rating to face-to-face interaction, followed by mentoring and coaching. Interestingly, no one picked online training or being provided with relevant reading, even though this might make the learning more flexible. These findings are supported by other research which shows that millennials in particular want to be mentored and coached (Barrington and Luetchford 2019; Holmberg-Wright et al. 2017).

While the research done by our university students clearly showed that for millennials, face-to-face interaction was essential and online leadership development does not work, some of the HR professionals we interviewed felt that online training will become more sophisticated, with even soft skills such as emotional intelligence and conflict handling being developed online.

Despite this, it is our view that the opportunity that these platforms provide to broaden access to the fundamentals of leadership development is one to embrace. Clearly, from other comments we have made in this chapter, such platforms do not lend themselves well to vertical and collective leadership development.

While we have outlined some of the advantages and disadvantages of different channels of leadership development, we know that commercial opportunity will also drive the prominence of some forms. Online platforms provide scale of access, relatively low cost per head and good margins for suppliers.

However, in the end, leadership development is ultimately about how effectively we help leaders grow. Coming back to where we began this chapter, leadership development channels need to embrace the fundamentals of learning. Suppliers of leadership development need to ensure that the methodologies they use drive people all the way through the learning cycle.

What Might Get in the Way of Change?

In any change context, you should also ask for good reasons why change does not happen. What needs to be unlearned?

The Illusion of the Perfect Leader

The idea of the perfect leader who delivers the definitive solution is probably what all organisations, systems and countries dream of. Although not explicitly, reading between the lines, this is also what leadership development suppliers often promise to provide. While we have seen in the history of leadership development that ideas about what makes a 'perfect' leader have changed over the last century—from being the person who knows best to being authentic, handling paradox, being responsible with foresight, resilient and being able to show vulnerabilities—we believe that unconsciously, the idea itself that a leader should be perfect has changed little. Rather, what we see is that the definition of 'perfect' has changed.

Several of the leadership development suppliers in our interviews mentioned the incredible pressure they see on leaders and felt that the idea of a superman/superwomen is still in people's minds. They critically reflected that now pressure is even higher, as this ideal person needs to be approachable, able to navigate a VUCA world, know when to listen, when to summarise, when to decide… in short, when to deliver the 'perfect' solution.

However, we have shown in the last chapter that this does not exist—the perfect solution does not exist in a VUCA world and, to be honest, it never existed. Unfortunately, for many decades, the consequences of leadership decisions were not seen quickly. Plastic was produced to solve the problem of cheap, hygienic and light packaging. Nobody could have predicted the plastic war which would one day fiercely endanger our well-being. Nobody predicted a cycle whereby one day this plastic would end up in oceans, eaten by fish and finally eaten by human beings again. Nobody understood the cause and effect of washing fleece jackets, which are so functional, would eventually heavily pollute our water, and that this in one form or another again would threaten our health and the health of our children.

System thinking is key in leadership development. Most of the leadership development suppliers we talked to, including ourselves, had been trained in system thinking in one way or another, helping to understand that complex events do not fit into a simple cause and effect pattern. However, while theoretically understanding that thinking systemically meant that any action had often unexpected consequences, the delay between one's action and the visible consequences of that action was often too long to be able to connect the dots across many years. This situation has changed due to many megatrends, including digitisation and globalisation. The mistake of a cook in Wuhan triggered in a very short time a global pandemic that no leader could have imagined.

So, it seems time to let go of the illusion of the perfect leader who knows best and navigates the organisation with wise strategies towards a shiny future. It's time to acknowledge that the only way to move forward is to recognise failure fast, analyse and then apply the new learning. The perfect leader who knows it all is an illusion which has become dangerous to believe in.

The Illusion of Knowing the Right Answer—Who Is the Expert?

In any traditional university setting, students are the learners and the professor is the expert—the one who has done the research, has read the books and has successfully added their own knowledge in the long stream of academic publication. Unfortunately, this is still the case in many business schools as well and therefore in many leadership or MBA classes. Why unfortunately? Because leadership is a 'living experience' and not a theoretical model where knowledge can be gained in diverse laboratory experiments. Leadership is, as Marshall Goldsmith once said, a contact sport (Goldsmith and Morgan 2006).

Reflecting on the outcomes of all our interviews and the unanimous agreement that in a VUCA world there are no simple leadership solutions, the illusion of the perfect leadership development supplier who is the expert and who is delivering the perfect solution is surely outdated. However, as most leaders have spent decades in settings where the teacher/trainer/professors have told them what was right (or wrong), the participants' invitation to the leadership development supplier to do the same is eve-present. Our experience shows that this is like a 'trap'—the minute a leadership development supplier claims to know the solution, the leaders will prove him/her wrong, quickly focussing on the flaw in the leadership development suppliers' arguments and pointing out that, as the argument is not flawless, the key message might not be right. In these situations, the leadership development supplier often feels the need to prove his/her authority and credibility which might lead to a contraproductive 'who is right' discussion.

Both of us have been in endless situations, especially at the beginning of our careers, where our credibility has been questioned with the underlying issue, 'Who are you and what do you bring that it is worth spending our valuable time here, that we listen to you?' In one setting, the HR professional even urged us to mention our connection to universities, dropping the names of other companies we had worked with, and encouraging us to share publications we had worked on if the content was related to the topic of the workshop we were running. The pressure for HR professionals to prove that they have found the best-in-class leadership development supplier increases the pressure for the leadership development supplier that indeed he/she is 'best-in-class'. In addition, the 'happy sheets' at the end of the programme, the wish to be invited again and of course every individual's need to be loved and respected also enhance this pressure.

While in coaching it is very well accepted to say as a coach, 'I don't know, let's explore together', it still needs immense courage to do the same in a setting with many senior leaders in the room. However, if this doesn't happen, change doesn't happen—a perfect leadership development supplier gets in the way of change. At the same time, it is not an option for the leadership development supplier to 'not know and be inexperienced', as then he/she won't be accepted as a catalyst for change. So, the facilitator as the leader faces the same challenge, the same paradoxes as being experienced and yet still a learner, being knowledgeable and also brave enough to step back—in short, being an expert and a novice.

Unfortunately, there is no recipe to follow, no clear instruction on what to do and what not to do. In a programme we have been running for many years, we have good proof of how the right balance leads to a desirable 'collective leadership'. This happened across several countries and included vertical leadership development for the individuals where we truly felt that participants did not consume but contributed, developed and grew together as a cross-country team. Pleased with this result, we used the same design the following year and the learning did not take place as expected. On the contrary, the participants fell back into a consumer attitude, judging the programme, the facilitator and the setting, and as a result collective leadership did not take place to the extent that we wished for. Why? Perhaps the reason was that the group was larger, the room we were using was less cosy and the acoustics did not work well, the weather was not as pleasant as the year before... or maybe we as facilitators did not get the right balance between being knowledgeable and being brave enough to explore.

From Consumer to Contributor

Often textbooks speak about the active learning experience or the active learner (Carnall and Roebuck 2015), ideas which still create the illusion of one who knows and can teach the other. So the better and more entertaining the mix of learning tools the one who knows uses, the better the leaner's learning experience.

During our time in leadership development, a question that has remained to a large degree unanswered is how to shift leaders from a consumer mindset to becoming an active leader of their own development.

Let us describe an all too familiar pattern. An early conversation on a development workshop with a delegate would suggest that they have little understanding of the content of the workshop or even why they have been asked to attend. The conversation then evolves into the practical space: 'Is

is quite noticeable that most evening speakers, facilitators of larger workshop settings, as well as leadership trainers, are often male, even though you might find many female coaches. While we can guess at some of the reasons for this, we have noticed that the HR (female!) professionals might often think that it is safer to choose a male facilitator, trainer, evening speaker, because most of the participants would be male. On the coaching side, we have heard other assumptions that male leaders might find it easier to open up to female coaches in a one-to-one setting, being more able to talk about vulnerability and emotions. Of course, neither the statistics for the above observations are available, nor any confirmation of what HR professionals have shared with us, but looking at the patterns observed, it is definitely important here to reflect on the danger of unconscious bias and stereotypes.

Keeping It Way Too Safe

Many leadership development classroom/workshop settings are incredibly predictable, for both those leading and those participating. This begins when the joining instructions are sent out—they include the logistics, agenda and possibly a few warm-up questions. The participants know the structure, and to a large extent the experience, in advance. Some are already planning when they can catch up on emails and when they can make that critical conference call.

In a way, this is counterintuitive to what it takes to really learn. Learning requires people to be in a curious state of mind. It requires people to be stretched out of their comfort zones.

CCL in their excellent paper (Petrie 2013) on 'vertical development' suggest that a critical element in what helps people really grow is 'heat experiences'.

How do we give people coming on development workshops enough psychological safety that they will take risks and hence grow? The typical leadership development workshop is not set up in a way that disrupts and disorientates. So why does this happen?

The tendency to keep it way too safe is driven by a number of factors. Starting with those buying the intervention, typically an HR/learning and development person, they need to be able to sell the intervention to their boss and the rest of the organisation. Normally, this involves demonstrating how they will measure success and, in a sense, outcomes.

Learning objectives are written for the group as a whole, and evaluation sheets are built on the back of this.

The supplier of the learning intervention is then briefed on these elements. They, in turn, design something that will meet these criteria. So, making people coming to the workshop feel safe and comfortable at the beginning is a good step in the direction of achieving these precious evaluation scores.

Suppliers know that if they do not hit that magic four out of five on the typical evaluation scale, they are unlikely to be hired again. Being hired again is of course a huge driver for many suppliers. In our view, this is an unhelpful starting mindset. Instead, the starting point should be how to design and deliver a development experience that the client needs, which at times may feel very uncomfortable.

That is the huge difference between what participants *want* in the moment vs. what they in fact *need*.

A key finding from our research interview questions to leaders was that it was often the development experiences where they felt uncomfortable at the time which they now look back on as being the most impactful. So how can HR teams/suppliers build partnerships which have enough trust between them to build these stretching, uncomfortable development experiences? How, in turn, can HR build enough trust with their organisational stakeholders to hold this space? This reminds us again of the occasion when one of us brought her skills and training as a psychologist to an intervention where these were welcomed as an opportunity to say the unsayable (see Chapter 2).

This is not a new concept. It is very much reminiscent of the jester at court, of the person who was invited and allowed to jokingly say the truth—and, depending on the king's or queen's personality and mood, they took a big risk in doing this!

What Else Gets in the Way?—Busyness

Busyness has become a badge of honour in many organisations. HR/suppliers start their design of leadership development interventions from a point of negotiation. How can I convince the organisation that this is really worth two days of their time? How can I convince them that they should stay off their mobiles and focus on what we are talking about?

In the aforementioned report, CCL mention the importance of 'elevated sense making'—in essence this is about how we design interventions in a way that build a reflective space to make sense of their experiences. Kolb, in his work on the learning cycle (Kolb 1984), points to the importance of building experiences that drive people right through the learning cycle—experience, reflection, theory and planning.

A lovely quote that a colleague of ours uses states that 'true reflection can only take place in still waters' (Taoist proverb). Participants often come to workshops busy and distracted. That busyness, as well as being a badge of honour, is often a habit. This is typified by a recent workshop experience. We had spent the first hour and a half of a development workshop getting people settled into an exploratory mindset and uncovering some of the big organisation issues that needed to be worked on. We called the first coffee break. At the mention of coffee, a participant to our right immediately took out his mobile and checked in with his operational team. One of his colleagues asked him why he was doing this. Was there a major issue back at base? The mobile phone user replied, 'Nothing big, I just like to check in'. A normal and understandable response, but the deepening of the reflective space was cut short.

In our experience, it often takes people time and a concerted effort from those facilitating to build environments where people unwind from this busyness.

What Else Gets in the Way?—Hierarchy

Our experience of how leadership development interventions are set up in organisations is driven by hierarchy. People of a certain grade are grouped together. There is safety in this—these are my peers. Participants will not have to explore their leadership with their bosses or subordinates present. Yet, are these not the people that often experience the real impact of their leadership? A memorable workshop experience was when a leader of a team offered to leave a workshop for a while so people could have a 'real' conversation about what was going on. Sharing these insights later with the leader was safe and powerful—for the team and the leader.

How do we build experiences that bring together all the relevant people to the leadership development conversation, regardless of grade? We feel that the strongest interventions are the ones which work on key organisational challenges, while building personal and collective leadership capability at the same time.

So often the final conversations of workshops are about how to engage the people not in the room in our conversations. Someone is entrusted with the flipchart output and reassures the others that they will disseminate it in some form to people of other grades.

Perhaps the first question in designing development experiences should therefore be about who needs to be involved in this organisation to really shift.

* * *

Hopefully, by examining some of what might get in the way of leadership development, we have not been too negative. Our intention is simply to clear the way forward, so that the frameworks we have suggested that will guide the future, and the tools that are available to facilitate this progress, can be more easily implemented.

References

Argyris, C. (2002). Teaching Smart People How to Learn. *Reflections: The SoL Journal, 4*(2), 4–15.

Barrington, S., & Luetchford, R. (2019). *Leading—The Millennial Way*. London: SPCK.

Bell, E., Bryman, A., & Harley, B. (2019). *Business Research Methods* (4th ed.). Oxford: Oxford University Press.

Ben-Hur and Ringwood. (2017). https://www.imd.org/research-knowledge/articles/making-generational-differences-work-what-empirical-research-reveals-about-leading-millennials/. Accessed 12 January 2020.

Boston, R. E., & Ellis, K. (2019). *UPGRADE: Building Your Capacity for Complexity*. London, UK: Leaderspace.

Carnall, C. A., & Roebuck, C. (2015). *Strategic Leadership Development: Building World-Class Performance*. London: Macmillan Education, Palgrave.

Clance and Imes. (1978). https://paulineroseclance.com/impostor_phenomenon.html. Accessed 12 November 2019.

Eigel, K., & Kuhnert, K. (2017). https://blog.matrixlms.com/vertical-development-or-why-leaders-thrive-on-experience/. Accessed 12 March 2020.

Goldsmith, M., & Morgan, H. (2006). Leadership Is a Contact Sport. *Content Management* [online] (pp. 71–79). Available at: https://www.marshallgoldsmith.com/articles/leadership-contact-sport/. Accessed 16 May 2020.

Hieker, C. (2019). Millennials at Work. *Coaching at Work, 14*(1), 43–45.

Hieker, C., & Rushby, M. (2017). Diversity in the Workplace: How to Achieve Gender Diversity in the Workplace. In B. Christiansen (Ed.), *Handbook of Research on Industrial and Organizational Research in the Modern Workforce*. Hershey: IGI Global.

Holmberg-Wright, K., Hribar, T., & Tsegai, J. (2017). More Than Money: Business Strategies to Engage Millennials. *Business Education Innovation Journal, 9*(2), 14–22.

Kegan, R., & Lahey, L. L. (2009). *Immunity to Change: How to Overcome It and Unlock the Potential in Yourself and Your Organization*. Boston, MA: Harvard Business Review Press.

Kolb, D. (1984). https://www.simplypsychology.org/learning-kolb.html. Accessed 12 February 2020.

McGuire, J. B., & Rhodes, G. (2009). *Transforming Your Leadership Culture*. San Francisco: Jossey Bass.

Microsoft News Centre Europe. (2018). *Reverse Mentoring: How Millennials Are Becoming the New Mentors—Microsoft News Centre Europe* [online]. Available at: https://news.microsoft.com/europe/features/reverse-mentoring-how-millennials-are-becoming-the-new-mentors/. Accessed 25 April 2018.

Moules, J. (2020). *MBA Students Demand Tuition Fee Refunds Over Campus Closures* [online]. Ft.com. Available at: https://www.ft.com/content/d093664c-0381-487f-99e6-027230e2104f. Accessed 15 April 2020.

Peterson, D., Hicks, M., & Peterson, D. (1996). *Leader as Coach*. Minneapolis, MN: Personal Decisions International.

Petrie, N. (2013). *Vertical Leadership Part 1: Developing Leaders for a Complex World*. Colorado Springs, Colorado: Center for Creative Leadership.

Revans, R. W. (1982). *The Origin and Growth of Action Learning*. Brickley, UK: Chartwell-Bratt.

Rooke, D., & Torbert, W. R. (2005). Seven Transformation of Leadership. *Harvard Business Review, 83*(4), 66–76.

Snowden, D. (1999). Liberating Knowledge. In *Liberating Knowledge*. CBI Business Guide. London: Caspian Publishing.

WHO. (2019). *Mental Health in the Workplace Information Sheet*. https://www.who.int/mental_health/in_the_workplace/en/. Accessed 16 March 2020.

CHAPTER 5

Key Takeaways

Abstract This chapter offers the reader the author's key takeaways from this book/research project. An anchor point for the future will be that leadership development addresses all five layers of the onion model—helping leaders grow to work at personal, team, organisational, industry and world levels. It is reflected how the leadership development industry will need to change to address the evolution in attitudes and behaviour that megatrends will bring. There is an acknowledgement that, in the light of megatrends, the channels through which leadership development is delivered will change. Importantly, this chapter also describes what will stay from the existing approaches to leadership development. Certain methods such as coaching and action learning are successfully used now and it is believed will meet the challenges of the future.

Keywords Complexity · Sense making · Channels of leadership development · Values · Uncertainty

Our experience of arriving at this set of key takeaways has been a fluid one. As such, this represents an attempt to consolidate at a specific in time.

As we re-read the main body of the book, we are struck by the way that our thinking had developed over the last eight months or so. A huge global crisis had of course heavily influenced this.

C. Hieker and J. Pringle, *The Future of Leadership Development*,
https://doi.org/10.1007/978-3-030-53544-5_5

Leadership development is a broad church of contributory experiences—people's work and life experiences, formal development workshops, advice from family and friends, formal coaching and mentoring, personal reading, etc. In a sense, many of those contributory experiences will continue to influence how leaders develop in ways which are highly personal and are hard to control. So these takeaways are more about the formal interventions that leadership development makes moving forward.

Five Layers of Leadership Development

Our earliest breakthrough in our thinking came with defining the breadth of what leadership development has to cover. We have represented this in our model of the five layers of leadership development: personal, team, organisational, functional and responsible leaders in the world. We believe that future leadership development interventions will need to address all of these layers to be truly effective. In the past, much leadership development has focussed on the first two layers of personal and team, only looking at organisational a little and even more neglecting the wider context. This needs to broaden to a focus on the functional and responsible leaders in the world layers as well.

Disrupting the Disruptor

A second key learning was a phrase that we came back to time and time again: 'disrupting the disruptor'. Leadership development is intended to develop people's thinking. Often, in order to do that, we need to disrupt their existing thinking. This is only really possible if, at the same time, leadership developers are disrupting their own thinking. If we as leadership developers become too comfortable and habitual in the way that we design and deliver interventions, we will be at odds with our clients. It is our view that suppliers of leadership development will need to come out of their comfort zones and take more risks in how they work with clients.

Megatrends

Thirdly, we started by asking the question how megatrends would shape leadership development works into the future? We deliberately did not have a fixed list of megatrends that we were applying to our conversation.

However, certain ones surfaced time and again in our discussions and the research interviews with others.

Digitisation, heightened by the way that people are being forced to work during the COVID-19 outbreak, will change how leadership development is delivered. Face-to-face gatherings will only happen where there is a very clear value-add by using this method—these will probably include development work such as coaching, action learning and team-based coaching. Digitisation will also lead through its broader access and lower costs to a greater democratisation of leadership development, moving it from the preserve of those near the top of the organisational hierarchies to being available to all. This is crucial, as current thinking is that leadership is something that all their employees and partners need to bring, no matter what their job or grade.

Individualisation—the sheer volume and ease of access which individuals have to quality leadership development material—means that motivated leaders will build their own personal curriculum for leadership development. The leadership development suppliers of the future will be the ones that can guide leaders through this material. Suppliers will also play the role of connector and convener, bringing leaders together either physically or virtually to allow them to share and grow further.

Demographics and changing societal values—leaders who are emerging in the workplace—now embrace the need for work that is aligned with their values. They want to feel that the organisations that they work for have a sense of purpose and are making a responsible contribution in the world. Leadership development will need to do more in helping leaders grow that responsible leadership layer. How do we help leaders build their own sense of purpose and values from which to navigate their actions, which will impact the global eco-system?

The physical and mental energy that leaders will need to build and maintain to cope with this VUCA world will increase. Leadership development will need to play a more active role in supporting leaders in these spaces.

A VUCA World

In a world that is becoming increasingly VUCA, leaders will need to be able to handle huge amounts of uncertainty and complexity. How we help leaders grow vertically, i.e. building the way that they think, will be hugely important.

Given the complexity and scale of many of the leadership challenges for the future, no single leader or organisation will deliver lasting outcomes on their own. Leadership development must help leaders grow the skills and mindset that will allow them to lead effectively in the collective leadership space. This will include enabling leaders to embrace diversity and quickly build trust with others.

As shown in the history of leadership development, it very much means handling ambiguity—the 'A' in VUCA. Handling the leadership paradox, or as Fitzgerald puts it more eloquently, 'The test of first rate intelligence is the ability to hold two opposed ideas in the mind at the same time and still retain the ability to function' (Fitzgerald 2020). This has always been, and will continue to be, a key skill and challenge for leaders. One purpose of leadership development is to support leaders to hold, reflect, breathe and live the paradox.

Channels of Leadership Development

Certain channels of more formal leadership development interventions will thrive, and some will fade. One-to-one coaching will continue to grow. Leaders will need that personal support, as they do their sense making in this increasingly VUCA world. Action learning and team-based learning will also thrive. Leaders will expect to develop while working on live organisational challenges, so there is less division between 'time away' for development and the 'real work'. Lectures driven by PowerPoint with only small amounts of interaction will fade. People will come to action learning environments having read the theory, expecting that they will work with others, rather than just listening in a traditional classroom-based format.

This shifting of the channels will, in turn, lead to a change in the skills required of the leadership development suppliers. They will need to build high levels of facilitation skills. They will need to be conversant in a wide range of tools and be able to bring them in at the right moment—something very different from being highly practised in delivering just one theory or framework.

Packaging

The packaging leadership development as a three-part product (a piece of research, a good speaker and ideally some written takeaway) will probably remain because it is part of the 'safe pair of hands strategy' in leadership development. Senior leaders like to be entertained and learn something at the same time. A 'takeaway', as a reminder of what happened, is also always appreciated and gives leaders the opportunity to deepen the learning. In addition, HR professionals like to know the newest trends in leadership development and be 'up to date' with 'influencers' to show that they know what's going on in the market.

Measuring Return on Investment

Finally, as we indicated earlier in the book, the leadership development industry is massive, with a huge amount of money invested in it. Organisations on both the buying side and the supply side will need to work harder at providing effective measurement showing the return on investment. For too long, the industry has suggested that it's difficult to measure real outcomes. This will no longer be acceptable. All disciplines have had to become more accountable as information becomes more transparent—and leadership development will need to do the same.

Reference

Fitzgerald, S. (2020). The Crack-Up. *Esquire February 1936* [online]. Esquire|The Complete Archive. Available at: https://classic.esquire.com/article/1936/2/1/the-crack-up. Accessed 5 May 2020.

CHAPTER 6

The Book Has Finished… But Not Our Journey

Abstract This book was written in order to make a contribution to the leadership development industry and to achieve some personal sense making. Next to deepening the understanding of what experts in the industry see as key to making leadership development sustainable, it shows the importance that the three primary audiences for this book—leadership development suppliers, HR professionals and senior leaders—prevent themselves from slipping into dangerously comfortable routines.

Keywords Collective leadership · Responsible leadership · Disruption · Sustainability · Change

Writing this book together was itself an enjoyable journey which has helped us make sense of our many years in leadership development. We have also grown together as co-authors, sharing ideas, reflections, irritations and inspiring each other—up to a point that when we edited the book, we often couldn't remember who originally wrote which piece.

Our book aims to provoke thoughts and questions about the shape of leadership development moving forward. In order to do that, it became very clear to us that we had to tell the longer story of how leadership development has evolved. Stopping to consider the longer story has felt really important, as both of us have invested so much time and energy in our careers. Many times during the writing we reflected on why we

C. Hieker and J. Pringle, *The Future of Leadership Development*,
https://doi.org/10.1007/978-3-030-53544-5_6

were choosing to write this book now. Perhaps it was a coming together of two very different but complementary people at a given moment in time. Maybe we both felt space in our careers to pause and do this work, and maybe there was something about the next 20 years of our careers and wanting to feel like the work we were doing was purposeful. We are not sure that through the course of our conversations we arrived at one definitive reason.

However, it provokes the question about what causes any dedicated professional to stop and think about their career and their industry in a more holistic way. Some reading this might think that we could and should have been asking these questions of ourselves and our work a lot earlier into our circa 25-year careers. This is a sentiment that we would agree with!

As we stated at the beginning of the book, our sense of discomfort at habits that we had easily fallen into grew through the course of our writing. As we move forward, how do we prevent this pattern of becoming comfortable with whatever the new 'normal' for leadership development looks like? How do we continue to bring fresh disruption into our work?

As discussed in the big why, we wanted to explore the influence of megatrends on leadership development and were curious as to the outcome. However, we have to admit that we were thinking more about disruption, wake-up calls and how to meet the demands of the changes we were facing—or those that would come. What we were not aware of was that some megatrends had already quietly but significantly influenced leadership development, and that leadership development as an industry had reacted to these somewhat unnoticed. The reflection in the chapter about coaching—as to how the trend of individualisation and delivery on demand goes hand-in-hand with a growing population of silver-society coaches who are more flexible with their time to meet clients' needs—was a new insight for us.

Writing the history of leadership development was a bit like looking back at our own careers—connecting the dots from those theories, speakers and gurus we were often excited about and had used in our workshops, trainings and coachings, without even noticing that this was becoming a new leadership development trend, building up on another one, and thus setting the scene for a future one. We never intended to be comprehensive here, but it proved to be very powerful to step into the 'researcher' role, looking back from an outside perspective at our working lives as HR professionals and how they had evolved. We were surprised at how much has changed—as you might expect—in the last 25 years, but also how little we had noticed.

And finally, a very insightful lesson for us was triggered by the leadership development onion we developed. Consciously and unconsciously, we had focussed on our preferred layers during the many years of our careers. These were our 'comfort zone' layers, and not surprisingly, these were the layers where we positioned ourselves as experts, with the consequence of sometimes neglecting the other layers. However, in our role as leadership development suppliers, we challenge leaders to reflect, learn and position themselves on all five layers. So, truly what we expect from others we have to do ourselves as well. This insight helped us to move out of our 'comfort zone' layer, not just in the conversations we had with the leaders, but also in our roles as leadership development suppliers.

As a result, we now initiate more discussions on layers four and five—how the senior leaders could also contribute to take leadership in the profession and increase collective leadership.

Before writing the book—and admittedly before the pandemic started—we felt that collective leadership was a challenging and an important topic, but in the workshops we were running or in one-to-one coaching conversations, this reflection felt mostly fairly detached, as one is towards an intellectual challenge. This has dramatically changed for us—we are now passionate about collective leadership, up to a point that we need to make sure that we have not become patronising. We are aware that the 'heat-experience' of the COVID-19 lockdown contributed dramatically to our urge to raise awareness of this aspect of leadership, and perhaps over time the emotional aspect of this will weaken. However, the trio of vertical leadership development, responsible leadership and collective leadership seems to be a very helpful platform to continue integrating our facilitator/coach roles, probably for the rest of our careers.

Index

C. Hieker and J. Pringle, *The Future of Leadership Development*,
https://doi.org/10.1007/978-3-030-53544-5